COURAGEOUS WOMEN FIND STRENGTH DURING THE STORM

Fearless Women Rock Volume One

Compiled by

Dr. Missy Johnson

CEO, Fearless Women Rock LLC
and
BreakFree Coach for Women

Fearless Women Rock, Volume 1
Courageous Women
How to Find Your Strength During the Storm

Compiled by Dr. Missy Johnson

Copyright © 2018 Be Fearless Be Free LLC
P.O Box 316 Interstate 94
Belleville, MI. 48112
Website: www.askdrmissy.com

All rights reserved. This is a work of non-fiction. No part of this publication may be reproduced, stored in a retrieval system, or transmitted in any form or by any means—electronic, mechanical, photocopy, recording, or any other—except for brief quotations in printed reviews, without the prior permission of the author/ publisher.

ISBN-13: 978-0-9899802-9-6
Photography: Breann White
Cover Design: Melodye Hunter
Editing/Formatting: Gloria Palmer Walker

Dr. Missy Johnson can be contacted at:
Telephone: 313-279-8712
Email: askdrmissy@gmail.com
Website: www.askdrmissy.com
Facebook: AskDrMissy
Instagram: @AskDrMissy
Twitter: @AskDrMissy

DEDICATION

This book is dedicated to:

Every person who has experienced a life-changing event that caused them to say, "I am done! I can't do this anymore." This book is to let you know: Yes, you can, and you aren't alone any more. Fearless Women Rock is a covering to guide you through your storms.

Every person on my team who worked with me to make sure this Anthology was compiled with excellence.

Detroit's finest, Pam Perry and Sylvia Hubbard, for supporting me throughout the process as I launched Be Fearless Be Free Publishing LLC. They worked tirelessly with me in the late nights and early mornings.

My husband, Lee, and son, Mychael, who supported me in the vision and showed up at every conference.

Everyone who prayed for me and the project.

Last, but definitely not least, to my God, Who kept me in good health and sustained me during every near-death experience. Without Him, I am nothing. I learned to trust the Lord with my whole heart and lean not to my own understanding. Thank You, God, for directing my path to carry out this assignment and to bless every person who reads this book.

ACKNOWLEDGEMENTS

I would like to thank all the Fearless Women Who Rocked in this book. I heard the voice of God and the cry for women to share their story, and I obeyed. My arms are too short to box with God and I will leave a legacy of Fearless Women Who Rock worldwide.

Tanya R. Bankston: You have experienced many disappointments, but you trusted me to tell your story.

Denise Cochran: No one knows the many trials you've faced but God. Thank you being a part of the journey.

Michelle Curtis-Bailey: Grace and mercy follow you, and because of your love for God, He is rewarding you. Thank you for trusting me to tell your story.

Martha Dodd: You are the apple of God's eye. He knew you from a little girl, and now you have blossomed into a beautiful woman of dominion. Won't He do it? Thank you for being a Fearless Woman Who Rocks.

Kimbré Evans: Look where He has brought you from, and you are shining like a diamond. No one knew but God. Thank you! Many women are waiting on you.

Staci A. Jackson Smith: Wow! I believe God sent you to me by air mail. Your faith carried you through this process. I am honored to have you on the journey.

Whitney Johnson: Since day one, we were connected, and look at you now. Your ministry is so powerful and so much more to come. Love you to pieces.

Lisa Yvette Jones: Powerful beyond measure. God has been speaking to you for a while. It's your time. Thank you for trusting me in this journey. It is an honor.

Carla Miles: Never give up. This is your story after all-the-hell you've been through: You never gave up. There is so much more in store. Thank you for trusting me with your story.

Lavonia Perryman: Wow! I am honored to have you on this project. You are a pillar in the political arena and a pillar in this book. I am so excited to have you in this book. Thank you for trusting me.

Brenda Puckett: You have been with me since day one. I told you that you have a story to tell and it's your time. Trust is big for you and I am honored to have you with me on Fearless Women Rock Volume I.

Shurvone Wright: I thank God for you so much. It is an honor to share your story. You will encourage so many women. Thank you for trusting me with you story.

TABLE OF CONTENTS

COURAGEOUS WOMEN: HOW TO FIND YOUR STRENGTH DURING THE STORM

Fearless Women Rock Volume One

THIS GIRL HAS A CALLING ON HER LIFE, SO LEAVE HER ALONE!

by Dr. Missy Johnson,

Author & Lead Facilitator

Growing up as a church girl from Detroit, everyone would say, "That's the girl from Motown with the Motown sound." I would be thinking, 'No, that isn't me,' but never would say it out loud. Detroit is best known for being the birthplace of Motown Records, where Stevie Wonder, Diana Ross, and the Jackson Five got their starts in music. These are just a few of the successful artists who became legends in the long tradition of the Motown-music era. However, growing up in Detroit, that wasn't my experience. So, when people made those comments about the Motown sound, I was kind of dumbfounded because I didn't know who or what they were talking about.

My experience was being in church Sunday and Sunday night. Tuesday night Bible study, and on our knees praying before it started. Wednesday night, choir rehearsal, and Thursday night, practicing singing parts; I was the soprano. Friday night service, and on Saturday night, one last rehearsal before the Sunday morning service, singing in the choir, or being a youth usher or junior nurse.

As I grew older, I was sick and tired of all that church. Every time they asked me a question in "Purity Class", a program for young ladies thirteen to eighteen, I was the one who disagreed the most with the teacher's responses. I would say, "Show me in the Bible where it says that." Or, I would say, "That's a lie; that isn't how I understood it." My questions challenged the teacher, and I was later pulled to the side and told to let the others respond; I was disrupting the class. The problem was, no one was responding, and I had to sit there and listen to this mess. I stopped going to the class. I was still in church, but I started doing my own thing so I wouldn't have to sit there for nothing—like, walking to the store to get candy, or doing my homework at church.

From that point, adults and even my parents started saying I was causing conflict at church, and I should be quiet and keep my opinions to myself. Yes, I got angry because I had so much in my heart, but I couldn't share it without being ridiculed. That was when I started believing no one would hear my voice. No one at home and no one at church would know I had something to say. I began losing value in who I was, feeling I wasn't good enough. Yes, I knew how to show up and be seen, but that was as far as I would go. I continued to attend church because that was expected of me as a minor.

One day, I went to church, and they were praying and walking around the church—and yes, I went with an attitude. A few church ladies tried to tell me I shouldn't be like that, but there was this one old lady I will never forget. Her name is Ida Barnes. She went to the ladies and said, "Leave her alone. As much hell is in her, she's going to be somebody one day." She told those church ladies, "Many are called, but few are chosen, and that girl has a calling on her life, so leave her alone."

She didn't hug me or anything after she said that. She just looked at me and kept walking and praying, and those church ladies left me alone. I thought immediately, *'She is the only person who gets me.'* That was a life-changing moment for me. *'I am chosen,'* I thought. *'Wow! "Many are called, but few are chosen, and that girl has a calling on her life, so leave her alone." Maybe one day, I will fully understand that.'*

It was a bright, sunshiny day and my phone rang. It was about Ida Barnes. My mom was calling to tell me Ida was dying. She had been sick for a while and not talking. However, on her deathbed, she told them she needed to see me. She called my name, Missy. I was scared because I didn't desire to see her like that, but because she had impacted my life so much, I had to get there. Unfortunately, it was too late. Ida Barnes passed while I was en route.

After her funeral, people asked me, "Why did she ask for you and she wasn't even talking? Do you know what she wanted to tell you?"

I said, yes, but I didn't share it with them.

After her passing, my personal life spiraled out of control, but professionally, I had it all together. I encountered many events in my personal life that almost killed me: marriage issues, near-death experiences, several members of my family dying every six months for two years straight, and family issues. Then, I had a career breakdown that caused me to just want to check out of here. Check out meaning leave everything and everybody behind. You see, I am considered the rock of the family and everyone looks to me to fix everything. I needed fixing, but I had no support for myself. The thing that kept me was my Faith in God and Ida's words: Many are called but few are chosen. That girl has a calling on her life, so leave her alone.

It has been years since the passing of Ida Barnes, who so greatly impacted my life. The strangest thing was we never talked that much, but she was always watching me from a distance. It was like she was my angel of protection.

Another person was my Aunt Mattie Jackson. She and Ida were great prayer partners and prayer warriors in the church. With these women, I could be myself. With Aunt Mattie, I could talk to her and tell her how I felt, but because she had so much going on, I never went really deep; however, she was my best friend. I called her my Harriet Tubman. She also passed and I was the last person to see her.

Those two passing left me empty, but somehow, I knew I had to do something impactful to honor these women. Even in my storm, I found the strength to start the Mattie Jackson Scholarship Program. It was a program for high school students to assist them with college funding and mentorship as they prepared for college, a program that kept her legacy alive. I started it with no funds, only faith. I was able to send over eighty-five students to college with money and basic needs for their first year of college. It was a very successful program until I got sick and almost died. Since I was the spearhead, the program went into hiatus and no one stepped up to take it over. It hurt me really bad, but I knew my job wasn't over. Again, all I could hear was Ida saying, "Many are called, but few are chosen. That girl has a calling on her life, so leave her alone."

Now what, God? I have suffered many things in my life and experienced many storms. What's next for me, God? I said three things to Him while I was in my storm: What You want me to do, I will do. What You want me to say, I will say. Where You want me to go, I will go. Well, the next event that happened was the diagnosis of cancer. I was pissed now! I thought I'd already paid the price with everything I'd been through prior to the cancer. After being pissed and playing Jasmine Sullivan's song, *Bust The Windows Out Your Car,* I asked God to forgive me. "Since You allowed this to happen, I will carry my cross in this storm."

This wasn't just any storm, it was a Tsunami. It was designed to kill me for real, but in the midst of the storm, I heard Ida's voice: "Many are called, but few are chosen. That girl has a calling on her life, so leave her alone." God told me, "That storm wasn't designed to take you out, but to take you up." God told me He needed me to be a vessel for women who needed to come out of their storms to tell their story. "You are the vehicle I will use to help women tell their stories. It was never about taking you out, but taking you *through* your storm." God told me He knew He could trust me, but I didn't know He would test me.

Today, I am cancer free. The journey has been overwhelming, but I never felt like giving up. I am honored God chose a church girl like me to help women tell their stories. My goal is to have one thousand women tell their stories so they can help others break free from the things that hold them in bondage. I am a girl from Detroit, and my Motown sound is: Amazing Grace, how sweet the sound that saved a wretch like me. I was once was lost, but now I'm found. I was blind but now I see.

Fearless Women Rock is a book about courageous women from around the country who trusted me to share their most-intimate stories. As the facilitator of this project, it has been a blessed experience to share this time with them. This book is designed to help other women reinvent, rebuild, and remember that life is beautiful and you will find strength in your storm. This is volume one, and if you are interested in volume two, we have room for you.

My personal coaching message is, **Trust the Process**, even when you don't understand. Pray about everything and please get a coach so you don't have to carry it by yourself. As you read these stories, I'm sure you will see yourself or a woman you know. I ask that you please share this book with another woman. Buy a few copies and give them as gifts. This is not another rock group, but a Fearless Women Rock movement. Please know, you are not alone. **Fearless Women Rock!**

Join our movement and please leave your comments on Amazon.

I am Dr. Missy, the lead facilitator of this project, and I encourage you to connect with the woman who resonates with you.

It is with great honor and humility that I share with you some of the most-powerful stories in the world. *Fearless Women Rock Volume I: Courageous Women Find Strength During the Storm.* This is a life-changing book that will break the stereotypes of women who feel they are alone in the struggles of life. It will encourage you to never give up. Quitting is not an option!

Meet the Author

Dr. Missy is the survivor of a sixty-miles-per-hour car accident, forty-seven days in a coma, and stage-three breast cancer. Dr. Missy answered the call of her audience to compile a book of the testimonies of other women who have turned their trials into triumphs. Fearless Women Rock Volume I is a compilation of testimonies from women around the country. It is a book about courage, commitment, and the celebration of how everyday women found strength during their storms. The stories of these women are powerful and will touch the cornerstone of your heart. These women are true Fearless Women Who Rock, the movement created by Dr. Missy Johnson.

Dr Missy is the CEO of Fearless Women Rock LLC, a platform created for women to share their courageous stories so they can leverage themselves to become speakers, coaches, and authors. Dr. Missy has been on the cover or featured in/on Speaker's Magazine, Power Network Conference, NBC, ABC, Huffington Post, and Marie Claire, in addition to many other media, radio, and television outlets. She is a John Maxwell certified trainer and recipient of the President Barack Obama Lifetime Achievement Award and the Michigan Chronicle Women of Excellence 2018.

Dr. Missy is an award-winning, international, two-time number-one bestselling author, speaker, and Break-Free coach with mastery in helping women reinvent their lives after they have reached a peak in their careers, through executive coaching and personal leadership development. Dr. Missy has a remarkable story and is considered by her clients to be a reinvention strategist for the GEN Xers and Baby Boomers. Dr. Missy's motto is: Become so unforgettable they can't forget you.

Dr Missy is also the author of the newly-released Fearless Faith, Life After Cancer: How to Survive a Life Tsunami and Win. She is married to her devoted husband, Lee. They share one son and reside outside Detroit, Michigan. Dr. Missy is available for speaking in the corporate arena and church events, and offers one-on-one and group coaching programs for women nationally and internationally.

Contact Dr. Missy at:

Website: www.askdrmissy.com
Instagram: AskDrMissy
Facebook AskDrMissy
Twitter AskDrMissy

FACE-TO-FACE WITH FEAR: HOW TO OVERCOME FEAR

by Carla Miles

At the age of forty-two years old, fear is what I faced daily. Fear had me stuck since the age of three years old. I can remember growing up as a child in Louise, Mississippi, walking in the park with my mother and hearing the stories of generational fears that plague the women in our family. I remembered how strong she was, always talking about her mother and the generations of things she'd faced growing up. Because of that, I believe the spirit of fear was deposited into me at an early age in my life.

One great fear I had was of dying. I never knew why, but I carried it into my adulthood. The other fear was of my mom passing, leaving me alone. Another fear I experienced was of not graduating from high school. I became afraid of people calling me dumb or stupid because I couldn't talk or write like them. Heck, I could barely understand what I was reading.

With no direction or guidance, somehow, I became a victim of sex trafficking. There are too many details to tell at this time, but what I can tell you is that it is the most degrading thing a female can ever experience in life. At the time I was involved twenty years ago, I had never done drugs or anything. It was horrific—always taking off my clothes for money and *I wasn't getting paid.* I was a sex slave without my permission!

One day, someone told me about God and I really started seeking him. Eventually, I was able to escape the madness when the people were busted. Yet, I still had scars from being a victim of the crime. A scar of contracting HIV from a man I didn't know. Yet, because of my faith and prayers in God, I have been HIV negative for the last ten years.

Another scar, from having had twelve abortions, was the fear of not being the greatest mom ever to my sons, Daniel and Adam. It was grace that kept me after all those abortions.

Last, but not least, was the scar that caused my fear of writing this chapter. My deadline had been up, but I was too afraid to send it in because I have problems with spelling and using the right words. I sent it over to my friend to help me get it together, but it was still incomplete. God told me to keep going, even after I missed the deadline. I told myself, "I am going to write my part no matter what!" I had to speak an affirmation over myself. I told myself to decrease and allow the Spirit of Truth to rise up in me so I could complete this chapter.

Well, here I am, Carla Miles. I overcame my fear of writing because Dr. Missy spoke into my life right at the time I needed her most. She wasn't aware of my fears or the pain I'd carried from a three-year-old little girl in Mississippi. As Dr. Missy began speaking into my life, she gave me an assignment. She said, "Write your truth and I will help you." She spent time with me and helped me tell my truth. I didn't feel judged, shamed, or belittled. She helped me feel empowered about who I am and allowed me to start facing my fear of writing. I was no longer alone in this process. This had been a giant in my life, but I overcame. I went from taking baby steps to teenage steps to adult steps, and I conquered the fear of writing.

I speak to myself: I am an overcomer by the blood of the Lamb and the word of my testimony, which I must write to pull someone else through their fears. I decided to write my story for those who believe in me in spite of what they've heard or believed. So, now that I have written it, I am no longer stuck. I can relax and embrace my *perfections* and my *imperfections.*

What I have learned about overcoming the fear of death due to the passing of my mother is that we all are born and we all are going to die at an appointed time, but there is a preparation I believe every person has to do. Let me explain.

I didn't know my mother was preparing me for her death. The last two weeks of her life were unusual. We'd had our trials in our mother-daughter relationship, but those last two weeks before her death were beautiful. We had the best time ever in our lives. She allowed me to play in her hair, wash her feet, anoint her legs, and we laughed uncontrollably for days. At that time, she knew she was going to pass, but I didn't. All that time, she knew she was preparing me for her departure, but all the while, never crying. She kept her smile or her face.

When she passed, I read the eulogy at her funeral. It wasn't a service about death; it was a celebration of life. I can still hear her saying, "You did an excellent job." I can hear her saying she's proud of me for writing this chapter. I can hear her saying, "I sent Dr. Missy to you so you would no longer seek validation from others, but be true to who you are." I can hear her saying, "I have grandsons who are handsome and smart, and you are a great mother." I respond to my mother, "Thank you for the last two weeks we spent together. Not only were you departing, but you were preparing me for my journey of life."

Even though I am writing while in tears, I am no longer afraid of death because my mother was preparing me to never fear death, or anything, ever again. On Mother's Day, May 8, 2016, she said to me before she hung up the phone, "When I die, I want you to be very close to God and not fear death. Everyone has an appointed time."

What I want the person who reads this story to know is: Everyone has a start date and an end date, but do not fear death. Celebrate life daily. Appreciate the people in your life. Take care of your business. When my mom departed, all her business was in order. People will talk about you, even if your reading and writing skills are sharp. Ask God to send someone in your life to help you on your journey. At the age of forty-two, He sent Dr. Missy into my life. She keeps it real without ridicule. I know I have worried her, but she has been very patient but stern with me. Celebrate life and live life to the fullest potential. That's why I will always love my mother and be a Fearless Woman Who Rocks. I found my strength while in my storm.

Meet the Author

Carla Miles is a motivational speaker, designer, author, actor, and an original cast member of Bravo TV's *Real Housewives of Atlanta.*

From humble beginnings, Carla was born and spent much of her childhood in the Catfish Capital, Belzoni, Mississippi, working side-by-side with her mom and stepdad, who were sharecroppers. Carla's backstory is the epitome of trial to triumph, overcoming domestic abuse, prostitution, rape, drug abuse, and other difficult circumstances that leave most broken. After many years of fighting to survive, and enduring tragedy and heartache, Carla mustered the strength to change her life by way of writing, designing, and traveling nationwide to speak against human trafficking.

She has participated in and spearheaded various charity initiatives to aid the fight against prostitution and human trafficking. She reaches many through using life principles and strategies learned through breaking the bondages and chains of her past.

To contact Carla Miles:
Email: cmmpwog@yahoo.com
Website: www.theformula3.com

... BUT I AM NOT CRAZY!

by Tanya R. Bankston

"You want me to do what?!" I raised my voice at my doctor. She said it again: "I am writing you a prescription for Prozac and Xanax."

"Prozac?! Lady, are you crazy?! This is what I get for coming to a white doctor! I am having problems with sleeping, mood swings, crying spells, isolation, weight gain, and night sweats. Crying over things that are insignificant is driving me crazy! I don't need medication for crazy people!" I said in frustration.

"Tanya, another option is for you to take hormone replacement drugs to help regulate your moods," she said.

"Doctor, when did you last read my medical file? I was diagnosed with Premenstrual Dysphoric Disorder back in 1990. The crying spells, mood swings, and my need for isolation started a long time ago. Now, they have gotten so bad, I can't stand myself! I don't like me! I get on my own nerves when it's time to have my menstrual cycle. My life is all messed up!

"I don't have a clue when my period is going to start! Menopause has really messed things up! At least before, I had signs that indicated my period was going to start, like breast tenderness or water-weight gain; now, I'm not getting the signals and my period just shows up, unannounced, at the wrong time! I can go from okay to rage in sixty seconds, and I feel as though this Incredible Hulk-type monster is going to tear everyone to pieces! Doctor, I can't control my moods!" I raised my voice in frustration.

"I can see you're having a difficult time with controlling your moods. These are your two options: take these pills or these pills. It's that simple!" This time she raised her voice.

Dr. Madison was a short, stout, older Caucasian woman who dressed in bohemian-style clothes. She reminded me of a throwback to the 1970's hippie movement. I thought, 'She did too many drugs in her heyday; that's her reason for prescribing these mood-altering drugs for me now.'

"But, Dr. Madison, I have heard stories of women killing their families as the result of taking Prozac, Xanax, and Ambien."

"Yeah, they were crazy, but remember, you aren't crazy, so there will be none of that," she chuckled.

"I fail to find the humor in any of this, Dr. Madison," I responded.

"I want you to come back in thirty days. That will be long enough for the medicine to get in your system and for us to determine if you're having any adverse reactions. In the meantime, try not to kill anybody,"

Wow, some bedside manner! It seemed as though she didn't understand my situation at all! But how could she understand as a white woman? She had no idea of the stigma associated with black people taking medicine for their moods! People understand taking medicine for high blood pressure and diabetes, but mental health!? No; not in my community. That's a no-no.

I rushed to the pharmacy to get my prescription filled. Now, my two weeks of "normal" were reduced even further. My silent suffering was increased to include shame and embarrassment associated with taking psychotropic medication. It was bad enough I'd worked so hard to keep my mood stable; now, I had to worry about taking medicine that could potentially make me crazy!

What is the pharmacist going to think? Will other people know I'm taking this medicine? What if the medicine makes me crazy? Is it going to change my chemistry? My mind was flooded with questions. My doctor hadn't answered any of my questions. In fact, she'd only added to my frustration! I was left to my own devices—finding information on the internet.

"Ms. Bankston, do you have any questions for the pharmacist?" the clerk asked. I casually glanced around the waiting area to see how many other people could hear our conversation.

"I don't have any questions; thank you," I responded.

"I just need to see your ID please."

I thought, 'Ooooo, she wants to make this interaction longer and more embarrassing than necessary.'

"Why do you need my ID?" I asked. Now I was getting a little offended by this entire scene.

"One of your medications is a controlled substance."

She looked in the bag to explain to me which medication was controlled.

"Oh, yes, the Xanax," she blurted out and it seemed like her voice was on the loudspeaker.

'Did she just violate my HIPPA rights?' I thought in shame. 'Never mind; just give her the-damn-ID and get out of here!

I rushed home and went online to check the adverse effects of the newly-prescribed medications. But my first order of business was hiding the medicine from my husband! I pushed the medicine as far back in the cabinet as possible. This medicine was not going to be the topic of conversation at dinner tonight! I decided to conduct a thorough investigation of Premenstrual Dysphoric Disorder (PMDD) and the medications I had been taking to help ease the symptoms.

I was shocked when I discovered several things. First, PMDD is listed under mental illness and considered a mood disorder. I was having symptoms associated with my menstrual cycle. 'Why is that viewed as a mental illness?' Cymbalta and Zoloft are both antidepressants and mood-altering medications. I wasn't depressed. I didn't feel depressed. None of the classic signs of depression were there. The bottom line was, if I wasn't having a period every month, I wouldn't have these symptoms. I began to get sensitive to the words Premenstrual Syndrome Disorder (PMSD). Most people haven't heard of PMDD, but it is a severe case of PMS. I had been going through the devastation of its effects every month for fifteen years, only now it had become uncontrollable without medicine! I didn't understand how, prior to the onset of menopausal symptoms, I could control everything, but now there was talk of depression, anxiety, and mood-altering drugs.

I spoke to a friend who I knew had been taking the same medications for years and she was normal. I sobbed uncontrollably as I explained to Sandy that I didn't want to be seen as crazy, or actually go insane because the medication had chemically changed my DNA. (Looking back, I was so ignorant of the facts!) She calmly explained the importance of getting stabilized for now, and if I needed to stop taking the medicine in the future, then I had the right to stop at that time. There was something about the word stabilized that conjured up a picture of a patient in a mental health institution in a straitjacket that made me hysterical again!

Sandy reminded me of the need to remain calm and to empower myself with knowledge rather than being caught up in a lot of emotional ignorance. Sandy had been a mental health nurse for more than twenty years at the time of our conversation. I trusted her, confident that she was knowledgeable.

That night I took my first Prozac and Xanax. I was terrified! I went to bed wondering if my husband could see any difference in my mood, or any weird behavior changes. Honestly, I didn't have any negative side effects.

When it was time to go back to my doctor, our conversation was different.

"So Tanya, it's been over thirty days, and I didn't see anything about you killing anyone on the evening news," she said with sarcasm.

"Dr. Madison, I am pleased with the medication. In fact, I haven't felt this good in years!"

"Well what about your sleeping patterns? Are you getting asleep faster and staying asleep longer?" asked Dr. Madison

"The Ambien and Xanax taken together are too much for me. I can't seem to get up in the morning; I feel too groggy. I also find I don't need to take the medicine at bedtime because I go to bed too late. So how long do I need to continue taking this medicine?"

"You only need to take it until it doesn't work anymore, or your menstrual cycles stop for a full year."

"A full year? Oh my gosh! At forty-seven, that could be several more years..."

"Yes—or longer... In the meantime, today, I want to check your blood levels. We will cross that bridge of the medicine not working or negative side effects if those things happen. For now, focus on feeling better and if you need to speak to a therapist."

"What do I need to see a therapist for?"

I am a strong black woman. I have been through a lot and I can handle a lot! I don't need to lie on somebody's couch for them to charge me money to talk.

"It is always good to have a good therapist. In the meantime, I want to see you back in six months."

I left her office and thought, *Why do I keep going to her?! She doesn't understand what it's like being a black person! White people talk to therapists; Black people don't talk to therapists! We don't have the money to go whine to somebody about the problems in our community and get charged for just talking. It isn't cool to talk to a shrink! What would I talk to a therapist about anyway?! You can't tell white people nothing about what's going on in your house, or next thing you know, they'll be trying to take your kids away! Momma always said, "What goes on here in this house, stays in this house!"*

I had so much dialogue going on in my head. *'What would it hurt to talk to someone? I have health insurance and therapy is included in my coverage. What would it hurt?'*

I contacted my trusted old friend Sandy and asked her about therapy. I didn't know anyone who utilized a therapist on a regular basis. Sandy shared with me that she had been seeing a therapist for years, since the death of her father. I shared with Sandy that I had seen a therapist when my brother died. His death was so traumatic and I was so depressed that I'd had to speak with someone to help me shake the depression. There was another time when my ex-husband and I had gone to marriage counseling, but we'd still gotten divorced, so the therapy didn't work.

Sandy once again was my voice of reason. She said, "Tanya, your divorce was not the therapist's fault. Did you go on a regular basis? Did you do the things the therapist suggested to help improve the marriage? Did you take the therapy serious? Did you take your marriage serious, for that matter?"

"Well, Sandy, I never thought about those things. I guess I just assumed, since we got divorced, that it didn't work."

"So, you put the responsibility of a dissolved marriage on the therapist? What were your issues that you required therapy for in the first place?"

"Whoa, Sandy; there were so many... We had issues of drug abuse, communication problems, financial problems, and general problems with boundaries and respect."

Sandy laughed. "How many times did you go to therapy?"

"I believe we went to counseling about eight times,

before he got mad and stormed out the session."

"Really, Tanya?! You were married how long? You had all those issues and you expected a marriage miracle to be performed by a therapist? Sorry, Sis, I love you, but that isn't realistic."

"Well, Sandy, do you think I should see a therapist? I'm not sure what I would talk about."

"You would talk about the same types of things we talk about. For example, talk about the frustration of being a single parent. Talk about how angry you feel when the kids' dad doesn't show up and leaves them waiting—no call and no show—and how you have to pick up the pieces of their hearts every time. You could talk about the disappointment and rejection you felt after your recent divorce, and how you thought you would be married forever. Or, how you say you will never get married again."

"Sandy, but why would I pay someone, a complete stranger, to share those personal things with when I have you? What would a therapist say to me differently? Besides, you were there for me during each of events you named. I don't want some stranger judging me, thinking they are so high and mighty, or better than me. At least when we talk, we share! All a therapist would do is take notes, then go back to discuss my business with their colleagues and write some fancy report saying I have a mental problem."

"Tanya, honey, I need you to do your research. It isn't like that at all! You have been watching too much TV and you have the wrong concept! I know you take pride in being a strong black woman, but I need you to reframe your concept, so you can look at speaking to a therapist more as it's self-care to keep you emotionally healthy. Call your EAP program at work and get a list of some therapists in your network. Look on the internet or call their office. Go to an initial appointment. If you don't like the therapist, don't go back! Trust me, Tanya, you won't share your entire life story in one fifty-minute session."

I did exactly what Sandy advised me to do and sought a therapist. I tried a white male therapist, a black male therapist, a white female therapist, and a black female therapist before I made my final choice. Oddly enough, my decision wasn't based on race or ethnic background. My decision was based on the clinician being empathetic and having a sense of understanding of my life experiences I was sharing with her. I was able to let my guard down and share my story without fear of judgment and without fear of her contacting the police, or petitioning the court to have me placed in a mental institution.

Even more important for me, she did not undermine my identity of being a strong black woman. In fact, she empowered me, validated me, and helped me understand that I'm stronger now because I'm able to take a healthy inventory of myself and my emotions. I understand my triggers that can make me more emotional, and I now know I also have Seasonal Depressive Disorder.

It has been more than three years since I took the first pill. My mood is more stable, I still go to therapy, and I know **I am not crazy**!

While many struggle to keep their heads in the game, Coach Tanya Bankston helps clientele worldwide leap over hurdles and successfully cross the finish line—many times, with minimal sweat and tears. Out of the shadows of abuse, low self-esteem, and trust issues, Bankston pushes clients to discover and cultivate the leader within. Complete with her no-nonsense coaching style, zero tolerance for excuses, and passion for reinvention and repurposing, Bankston inspires women to transition from simple existence to living a life of abundance—unapologetically.

From the abandonment of her father, molestation, and date rape to domestic abuse, welfare dependency, and divorce, she's no stranger to the struggle. She's made a conscious choice to walk as a victor, not a victim. As a certified life, leadership, and solutions-focused coach, Bankston trains her clients to not only develop stellar products and services, but quality relationships—relationships that position them to stand out and soar in the marketplace.

In addition to her coaching certification from the Universal Coach Institute, she also holds a master's degree in Leadership, a bachelor's degree in Community Development and Health Science, and a graduate certificate in Human Resources from Central Michigan University.

Meet the Author

As the president and CEO of Greater Heights Coaching & Professional Development, LLC, Tanya encourages clientele to reach higher, achieve more, and live their best life now! Her signature team-building workshops have encouraged audiences from D.C. to Kansas City, offering them key tools on negotiations, collaboration, compromise, and communications. Founded in 2009, Greater Heights offers both corporate and team-building activities for business professionals of all backgrounds. Together with her educational background, corporate tenure, and passion to drive others to succeed, Tanya's on a definitive mission to positively impact the lives of all she comes in contact with—taking them from good to great!

Unlike the average life coach who coaches clients to become better at what they do currently, Coach Bankston encourages her clientele to throw the baby out with the bath water and reinvent themselves—opening the door to a myriad of opportunities. Just because a team has a coach doesn't mean they win. Let Coach Bankston catapult you to your next best level of success—fostering change through the pursuit of personal and professional excellence.

To contact Tanya R Bankston, Change Doula, helping

women give birth to their dreams, goals, and vision for speaking engagements or to schedule your next coaching experience:

Phone:866.733.3654
Email: coachtbankston@mail.com
Twitter: CoachTBankston
Twitter/Instagram: www.CoachTBankston.com

NOTHING LEFT TO LOSE

by Denise Cochran

"The secret of change is to focus all of your energy, not on fighting the old, but building on the new."
~ Socrates

I believe the things we experience in life are not just for us, but are to serve as tools to help inspire the lives of other people. In the corporate world, I have been a financial analyst, a business analyst, and procurement support engineer. In my newfound world as an entrepreneur, I am an author, a speaker, and a coach. I use my passion coupled with life experiences to assist others in discovering their purpose. I am also an advocate for mental illness/health, suicide awareness, and bullying/cyber-bullying.

Mental illness has touched close to home, and I have vowed to use my time and my voice to help remove the stigma associated with it. Helping to care for a sibling suffering from dementia and others suffering from mental disorders is challenging, but facing the reality of having a mental disorder of my own has been life changing. My disorder? Addiction.

Addiction

When we hear the word addiction, the most common things we think about are drug and alcohol addictions.

"Addiction is a condition in which a person engages in use of a substance or in a behavior for which the rewarding effects provide a compelling incentive to repeatedly pursue the behavior despite detrimental consequences." – Psychology Today.

In my family, some have struggled with alcoholism and a few with drugs. Witnessing the generational damage addiction has caused, I chose not to succumb to those things as I've watched it hurt, handicap, and destroy some of the people I love. I'm not saying I've never had a drink, but I can take it or leave it. I have friends and family who have recovered from drug and alcohol addictions. Fortunately, I didn't struggle with that; it just wasn't an option for me, period. However, I have felt like the addiction I suffered was worse, because although it wasn't a substance, it had an effect that took me to the same mental and behavioral places as substance abusers—a scary place that controlled my mind and my actions. My addiction? Gambling.

The Gambler, The Winner?

I considered myself a true gambler. I wasn't the kind who gambled and never won. I would gamble and win big, and I would win quite often. Just walking into the casino sometimes, I would sit down and win. My problem? I never could simply walk away after winning because I would be so caught up in the adrenaline rush. The whole time I was gambling, there was this inexplicable feeling, as if I were someone else. Those who understand this or can relate have at some point been addicted to something or know someone who has. Those who have never dealt with being addicted to anything won't quite understand what the big deal is. "Just stop," you say. "Just walk away." If only it was that easy.

There is a totally different world inside the casino. There's this exhilarating feeling you get when you are gambling—the winning, the atmosphere, and the fun. What started out as just fun became my place to relax—nobody bothering me or looking for me to do this or do that. It was my escape. Having VIP status was amazing with all the perks and celebrity treatment I got. In my mind today, it showed how foolish I was to have gained that status based on the amount of time and money I gave to the casino. Nevertheless, you have friends you've made there; everyone knows you. It's like having a family right there, doing what you like to do. They understood me.

As you are gambling, the need for more takes over. You know you should quit because you are ahead, but then you think, 'One more hand,' or, 'I will leave right after I play these last few chips.' Then, you're losing. You bet what was supposed to be your last bet, then you reach in your pocket and grab a few more chips to play this hand and you win. Eventually, you get sucked backed in because you now want to keep winning to get back what you previously lost. And the cycle begins.

Don't misunderstand. I have left the casino a major winner many times. I've paid bills, bought a few big-ticket items, splurged on my kids and myself, and even shared my winnings with family. You name it. As a gambler, you can best believe I took some of the winnings and went right back. Why? To do it again.

The Gambler, The Loser!

The side that many don't understand as being detrimental is the fact that there are losses too. It was in the moments right after losing that became crucial for me. The losses after being on a gambling high are dangerous. When you leave, having put everything on the table (or in the slots), you walk out busted and disgusted. You are now at your lowest. This low can lead you into depression, desperation, and even suicide. You're mad, you're irritated, just plain frustrated.

There's a lot to face when you step out to pick your car up in valet parking. You sit in your car feeling stupid, looking crazy. You look around in the car for change or those few dollars you thought you'd left just to get gas to make it home. Your mind is racing because you've messed up the rent money again. Your palms are sweaty because, not only do you have to still get up and go to work, now you have to figure out where the money will come from to pay the car note, the insurance, gas, even groceries. All because you deposited your funds into the Bank of Casino.

You can't tell your family because some of them don't know you gamble and others don't know to what extent. You can't face your children because when they saw you that afternoon (not knowing where you were going), you were happy, hopeful, and full of life. But, when you came back that night or the next day (yes, I said the next day), you are now tired, evil, broke, and don't want to be bothered. This behavior is much like the substance abuser who hasn't had their fix. You become a different person until you get your hands on some hope (money) to go back and get that fortune you just lost. Some gamblers chase the losses from the night before, some chase the losses from the week, from the month, and so on. Everyone's reason or strategy for their chase is different, but the mentality is the same. Is it for the money? Is it a dopamine high? Or a serotonin low?

Chemical Imbalance

I could go on forever about gambling. It is a very deep subject. Some of the chemical imbalances caused by drugs and alcohol are the same in gamblers. Lower levels of serotonin and higher levels of dopamine play a large part in the mental drive of gamblers.

"There is scientific evidence that addictive substances and behaviors such as gambling share a key neurobiological feature—they intensely activate brain pathways of reward and reinforcement, many of which involve the neurotransmitter dopamine."- Psychology Today

"Dopamine plays a big role in motivation and reward. If you've ever worked hard to reach a goal, the satisfaction you feel when you achieve it is partly due to a rush of dopamine. Serotonin is considered a natural mood stabilizer. It's the chemical that helps with sleeping, eating, and digesting. Serotonin also helps to reduce depression and regulate anxiety."- Healthline.com

Nothing Left to Lose

Gambling had a hold on me that I thought never

would let go, and for years it didn't. Once I accepted the gambling addiction, I was able to make the decision to let go of it. I finally arrived at a point where I had nothing left to lose. One day after fourteen years of gambling, I looked at my life and asked myself, "Why am I so unhappy with where I am in life? Intelligent, outgoing, talented, and such great potential. Why am I so broke and so broken? How did I get here?"

When I began to dig deep inside myself to understand where I'd gone wrong, I uncovered a lot of things that bothered me. I knew I had to face these things in order to change my life. I had to release guilt and anger. I prayed and asked God to help me brace myself for the uncovering, and to get my mind and heart ready to accept, understand, and adjust. It was time. A lot of my decision making, I began to realize, had been on impulse.

During my self-examination, I asked myself, "What is it I have dreamed of the most?" My answer was, "Having my own successful business, building wealth, and creating a legacy for my daughters." My next question was, "What do I feel is keeping me from my dream?" It was a lack of focus, self-discipline, and money. I looked at my casino win/loss statements from a few years prior. Let's just say I'd gambled enough to have funded more than two of my dream businesses. I had gambled away enough money to have financial security for my children if I was to leave this earth today. I realized I was my own problem. At that moment, I challenged myself to be my solution. I could no longer stay in such an unhealthy, stagnant state. I had absolutely nothing left to lose.

I thought about all the opportunities I may have missed out on and some of the effects my disorder may have caused.

1. Had I missed out on having my own business for being locked down at the casino? I thought about the time spent there, when that time could have been spent discovering and living in my purpose.

2. Had I missed out on writing a bestseller for being locked down at the casino? I thought about how my experiences could be so therapeutic and help someone who thinks they walk alone.

3. Had I missed out on my husband for being locked down at the casino? I thought about the relationships that had been tainted because of being preoccupied with gambling.

4. Had I missed out my financial blessings for being locked down at the casino? I thought about the financial woes that had been created. I am still recovering from them now.

5. Had I missed out on moments of time that I could have been enjoying with my children? I thought about the emotional damage I may have caused my daughters because of that habit, that choice.

Gambling addiction is now considered a mental-health disorder that is understood to be one of many kinds of impulse-control problems. Gambling may produce a level of mental ecstasy that encourages the gambler to keep repeating the behavior to achieve that effect. Similar to substance abusers, the gambler develops a tolerance for gambling which causes them to take greater risks to achieve that euphoria, regardless of the negative consequences. Pathological gamblers may be in denial about their behaviors and may not believe they have a problem at all.

Gambling was the name of the hurricane in my life and it created a path of total destruction. I finally came to the point of feeling as if I had nothing left to lose. It wasn't only losing financially, but physically, emotionally, mentally, and spiritually. I had felt the euphoria from gambling for so long, it had become natural. Quitting was just one of my fears. It wasn't the fear of stopping the act; it was the fear of who I would be without it. It was the fear of who wouldn't support me once I let go. It was the fear of having to face my loved ones and their disappointment. Do not be afraid to face your fear.

Facing the Addiction

"Change is not meant to be easy. Change is meant to be endured."
- Denise Cochran

When you trust in God, you can do anything! The saying, "The first step to recovery is admitting you have a problem," is true. Whatever your vice may be, your addiction, your reason, your excuse is in your life, you can come through it victoriously.

• **Recognize the problem exists.** You cannot seek to fix a problem if you don't recognize the problem exists. Identify and admit there is a problem.

• **Decide to change.** In order to change or get help, you have to want it. No one can help you if you don't want to be helped. Make up your mind that enough is finally enough; then do something about it. We all know the definition of insanity: You can't keep doing things the same way, expecting a different result.

• **Forgive yourself.** In order to move forward, you have to forgive yourself. Renewing your spirit while harboring a spirit of unforgiveness will leave you complacent in your process. You can't change what has happened in your past. Holding on to it only gives it more power.

• **Pray for forgiveness and guidance.** He forgives us even when we don't deserve it. He forgives us even when we don't know how to forgive ourselves. Go to Him; ask for His direction. He will guide you through your transitioning, but you must have faith. You must trust the process without question.

• **Seek help.** In any process you go through to make change, an important component is support. Support from professionals, your family, and your friends is not a sign of weakness. To seek help in a time you may be at your lowest point is actually an indication of strength and courage. Allow those who can help you to help you.

• **Develop a plan.** During your recovery process, develop a plan for how you will continue on your path of renewal. When you set short-term and long-term goals, you can monitor your progress and have something to reference if you start to get off track. Hold yourself accountable for where you are, or are not, on your plan.

• **Release whatever feels foreign to you, to your life.** The change you need for your life, only you can define. Change your mind, change your life. Do not worry about what other people may think or feel. The reward for letting go is far greater than the scorn of people who have no compassion for change. Oftentimes, the people who have negative things to say about you are only doing so to masquerade their own fears. The only thing that matters is what you think of you. Live your life for you.

"Your current situation is the result of your past decisions. If you are not satisfied, the future is your canvas. Create your masterpiece."
- Denise Cochran

Don't be hard on yourself. We are our own worst critics. Stay focused and determined. Remember, it is a process, so follow the rules and have faith with no fear. God made you to be victorious! Know that you are a Fearless Woman Who Rocks!

Meet the Author

Denise Cochran is an author, a speaker, and a certified life coach who decided it was time to live in her purpose. Successful in various positions throughout her professional career as a financial analyst and a business analyst, Denise came to the realization there was a need for change in her life. She understands that the things we experience in life are not only for teaching us, but serve as learning tools in the lives of someone else.

Denise finally gave up on trying to fit her entrepreneurial mindset into a corporate environment and walked away from Corporate America. She is the owner of Live With Purpose LLC, and Designs of Creativity, Graphics and Marketing Company. Denise is currently working to establish her non-profit, Can You Hear My Cry, as an advocate for mental illness, suicide awareness, and bullying. Her words of empowerment are, "Change Your Mind, Change Your Life."

To contact Denise Cochran:
Website: www.denisecochran.com

THE WOMAN IN THE MIRROR

by Michelle Curtis-Bailey

I looked in the mirror and didn't see the reflection I wanted to see. I saw puffy red eyes that were tired of crying, tired of hiding, tired of not being seen. I still can't believe I was that girl. While I have always shown up and had to be 'fully' present, I did it while hiding.

Yes, I was that girl—invited to events such as the baby shower, barbecue, bridal shower, etc.—who would show up and hide behind helping set up, getting food ready in the kitchen, or cleaning up. In an effort to avoid people, I hid behind doing tasks, because in doing, I felt needed. Resorting to doing was often the escape. The struggle was negotiating where I felt valued for who I was, not what I was doing. I often asked the question, "How can a confident person struggle with feeling valued?"

This struggle with value wasn't tied to my self-worth, but to my value in the eyes of others. The question of, "Do they want me for me or what I can do for them?" was the filter I used for the many circles I moved in.

We've heard it before in various settings that someone can be in a crowded room and still feel alone. My level of aloneness was wrapped in the cycle of busyness. How easy it was to hide in the midst of doing something that benefitted others. How easy it was to blend in, all because I was unsure of if what I had to offer was enough. While I wanted to be received for who I was, I only saw what I did as an exchange.

As a child and younger adult, I didn't really push the envelope, so I managed by avoiding drama, keeping to myself, and building a Fort Knox-like wall around my heart. Those walls, originally intended for protection, were hurting me in the long run. I thought, if I just did my best, showed up as I had taught myself, my work and presence would prove my worth. Oh, how wrong I was. After time, I saw that this issue of value wasn't so much a matter of worth to others, but something deeper. Using my works to define my value seemed innocent enough, but it was a symptom of an issue of the heart. Rather than being at the feet of Jesus, my heart was at the mercy of my false perceptions of others' receptivity of me.

I didn't want to be that woman who on the outside looks put together, but on the inside is personally struggling. Maybe with an innocent intent, but the real root of the struggle, distress, and uneasiness was pride. I was the doer. As a recovering perfectionist, I realize I'd stressed over my self-imposed value in the mind of others only being tied to what I did. I did not like what I saw when I looked in the mirror because the reflection was someone I didn't recognize.

Here's the thing though: This thing called pride isn't something I would be proud to shout from the mountaintop and say I struggled with this. Seeing the narrative of what I'd built in my own mind, it wasn't self-protection, it wasn't to avoid people, it wasn't to not be hurt. It was a subtle reliance on self-sufficiency that grew into rigid structure and order, manifested in thoughts like, 'I'll just do it so I know it's done right.' 'I'll help out so I'm not viewed as a spectator.' 'I'll take on the extra work because no one else was willing to step up.'

Initially, it looked like an innocent approach to support and get things done. But given there wasn't much middle ground with me, it was either one end of the continuum or another. I didn't function in humility of service, but in what I felt was an obligation to demonstrate my value. That was the end of an extreme that wrapped me in a cycle of consistently doing with great reasons to justify the insanity. Doing was my protection. The Fort Knox-like wall built around my heart was crystal clear. You could see me, but I wouldn't let you in. Similar symptoms of hiding behind work, functions, and service also had roots in a lack of trust.

Getting to the awareness that a lot of my value was based on what I did was the hardest dose of reality. It hurt to see the bleeding heart that somehow showed up in my weary eyes and heavy smile. The journey to overcome self wasn't a quick fix of just pray about it, read a book, acknowledge it, and move on. It was something where I had to see another side of the life I was doing, not living, and say to myself, "There has to be more than this."

My dear sister who is tired of doing, tired of running, tired of performing, tired of having to do it all: There is a place of rest on the other side of your busyness. It starts with being honest with yourself and taking full personal responsibility for where you are now and the choices that brought you to this point. You are not defined by what you do. Who you are is enough. The well-done makeup, the linger of Chanel No. 5, red bottoms on your feet, or the LV on your arm will never cover the places you choose to ignore. The corporate title and/or the letters that follow behind your name will not come to your rescue when the only thing to kiss your pillow at night is your warm tears. On the other side of the crazy schedule, the demands, the expectations is peace. Not some arbitrary illusion of what peace is, but real peace.

While at work one day, I happened to be thinking about the words of Amazing Grace. Tears began to flow from my eyes—without my permission, might I add—in a way that shocked me. I was singing the song in my heart and I got to the words, T'was grace that taught my heart to fear and grace my fears relieved. How precious did that grace appear the hour I first believed.

Grace. Grace. Grace.

What I needed to come to terms with was grace. Not perfection, not pride, not what I did, or what I could do, but grace. I slipped into my office, closed the door, and had one of the most-honest conversations with God I can recall. It dawned on me that pride was the root of my anxiety, my distress, my frustration with others, my lack of being fully present in my own life as a whole woman.

Being a woman of faith and a believer in Jesus Christ, I needed to confess that pride had worked its way into my heart. Yes, as believers, we are not exempt. Once you are aware of that, you cannot, however, remain there and wear [pride] as a brooch. While fully functioning on the outside, I had mastered human doing and missed a lot of the human being. For most of what I can remember, I was always striving for something. In high school, I couldn't wait to go to college. While in college, I planned strategically for life after college. After college, I did the things I wanted to do, little by little, checking things off my list. Could those checks have been a false sense of success to accomplish the items on my life checklist, yet miss the journey of what it took to actually get to where I am now?

It is now that I can look back at the level of intensity I approached my life with and say, "I feared losing control." That fear was the fuel for my very own control issues that I approached my work and service with. In my journey to being, I had to sit still long enough to observe the woman I was becoming. Beyond all the quotes and motivational sayings, I began to see the person of who Michelle was beyond the place of the circumstances, accomplishments, or even my own abilities. There is no way we can look outside and find an answer we are unwilling to look for within. This process of being came in the form of the investments in my own breakthrough: the investment of time, finances, relationships, books, counseling, and coaching in getting clear on my role and the things for which I am responsible. Little by little, I began to let go of what I could no longer control. Each step of this journey came with accepting my personal responsibility.

This journey in courage was one where qualification didn't come from any external factor but from within. I had to acknowledge where I was in God: that although I believed, I was having some real trust issues. Many times we allow negative experiences to define us. We sink so low that we don't see our own value. If the negative memories trap you, there is nothing anyone can tell you; you will remain stuck. God wants to create new memories. It's easy to get hurt when our expectations are too high and others don't measure up to them. Unfortunately, we hold others to those expectations and a level to which we aren't even willing to live up to. God is calling us to a new level of humility.

What I love about God is that He is a good Father. Through His Word, He begins to reveal who He is, who He says we are, and restore us to a place of healing and wholeness. When I looked back at the shape of my twenties, I saw a lot of my life was defined by what I did, not by who I was. The process to becoming whole takes the willingness to see who you really are, acknowledge your patterns of behavior, and taking the time to unpack it. Over the years, I have invested in my education, my financial development, spiritual development, and professional development. Outside of getting to know Jesus, my greatest discovery was getting to know myself through intentional personal development. In this journey, I saw that none of the challenges I'd walked through would be wasted experiences. As for me, so for you. There is nothing you have encountered that is too much, too terrible, or too defeating that you cannot bounce back from.

A few months ago on the way to church, it was a 'themed Sunday', so I expected a certain type of 'themed sermon'. Oh how wrong I was—again. On the drive, God began to deal with my heart, that it was time to forgive.

"It's time to release the very weight you've been carrying around for so long. It's time."

That same Sunday, the words the guest minister used were etched on my heart as he repeated himself about seven times, each time slower and with greater intensity. "The silversmith holds the silver in the fire until he can see his reflection in it." Could it be we are held in situations long enough for us to be aware of our impurities and junk so God can begin to make the changes in our life and set us free? That same week, after a little over three years of holding onto the wrong done to me, I experienced a release that was pure. It was as if God himself had said, "I've got this, Michelle. You can let it and the person who did it to you go for real now."

I saw and felt the damage of unforgiveness—physiologically, emotionally, and mentally. After releasing that hurt, something began to happen in my heart and mind. Taking keen awareness of my mindset and thoughts, I was able to reframe the lens and perspective that I made decisions through and see a reflection of the life I wanted to live. I wanted to live whole in mind, body, and spirit, and changes were needed to reflect that in my everyday life.

The choices to serve and contribute no longer come from a place of, "I have to do it," but instead, "I get to do it." My yeses are stronger because I'm able to take my whole self to an assignment, not a false humility of obligation. My noes are stronger now because I realize, though I may be able to do certain things, it doesn't mean I have to do it all. Recognizing my assignment in all I put my hands to helps me make concrete decisions I can stand on without fear, intimidation, or apology.

Now when I look in the mirror, I not only see my external features, I also see a heart that has been healed. A heart that now wants to be generous and overflow with love through intentional service to humanity. Taking personal responsibility for my purpose and assignment allows me to live a life poured out, and I believe that is God's heart for all of us. We don't have to live lives hidden behind masks, with self-defeating behaviors or deception. We don't have to isolate ourselves and do life alone. There is a God who is able to take you by the hand and usher you into His peace, wipe your tears, and gently remind you of who you are in Him. This God is able to heal the broken places of your heart you don't even want to acknowledge are there.

My dear sister, if there is residue on your heart, it will show up in your behavior. I pray you never get to the place of living with damaging behaviors of dysfunction to justify staying stuck. There is a place of safety in Him, that when you look in the mirror, you will see who God has called you to be. The beautiful and wonderfully-made you—in spite of your past, in spite of your choices, and in spite of who you even think you are. Who God has called you to be is greater than all you can ever say over yourself.

It is my prayer and declaration over you, that as you take the greatest journey inward, get to know the One Who wrote the script over your life and allow Him to usher you to places that your mind cannot even begin to conceive. His plans for you are greater.

This journey of self-awareness in my own personal growth and development has taken me to places of seeing glimpses of who God says I am. I trust that for the journey ahead, you too will know, honor, and appreciate the woman you see staring right back at you.

Meet the Author

Michelle Curtis-Bailey is a purpose-driven woman who is passionate about living a life poured out. A native of Brooklyn, New York, Michelle has earned a B.A. in Sociology and an M.S. in Student Personnel Administration from SUNY Buffalo State College. Michelle is a higher-education professional and strategist who continues to challenge others to maximize their education, life experiences, and potential as a tool for greater success and significance. Her objective is to impact a generation of individuals to be in radical pursuit of their vision, while cultivating personal responsibility, strategizing industry influence, and being whole in the process.

Michelle is also the founder/strategist of Education on Purpose, a college planning and career strategy company. As a contributor to the education industry, her feedback and engagement has been featured in US News and World Reports, Huffington Post, Washington Post, NerdWallet, and more.

To contact Michelle Curtis-Bailey:
Email: michellecurtisbailey@gmail.com

THE EVOLUTION OF A WOMAN OF DOMINION

by Martha Dodd

First, let me identify a woman of dominion. This woman understands the importance of maintaining her wellness, wisdom, and wealth. These are the three pillars of her life that, if she doesn't guard and protect them against life's unknown catastrophes, she and everyone she is responsible for or serves is severely impacted in one way or another. Today, I can say I have evolved to be a woman of dominion, and I have to give honor to my parents for laying a good foundation.

Born to Cuban parents in Brooklyn, New York, my father reared me with a strict hand and a mighty fist, while my mother guided me with compassion and tenderness. My upbringing in New York was bittersweet. My family, extended family, and community were Cuban, Jamaican, and American. We did everything together. We established businesses and supported each other. We went to each other's homes unannounced for breakfast, lunch, or dinner; we shopped in Long Island and The City; and every weekend, someone was having a party to celebrate a birthday, wedding, baby shower, or graduation. We attended church together, hung out at the beach, enjoyed boat rides, Bear Mountain picnics, or we just plain chilled at each other's homes.

I thoroughly enjoyed school and made excellent grades, thanks to my mom, who always encouraged and supported my eagerness to learn, and to my father, who wouldn't accept any grade lower than a B. Since my dad wasn't from this country, he learned the American way of business and finances. He learned quickly that he couldn't work as an employee, and he formed two businesses in New York, a Texaco service station and a painting contracting company with his eldest brother. As an entrepreneur, my dad was always following up on leads for his painting contracting business. Our family Sunday drives consisted of seeing a potential client, going to the amusement park, visiting friends or family, and dinner, then coming home to type the estimate on an old black 1920's typewriter.

When I started eighth grade, my dad advised me to take typing. By the time I hit high school, all my electives were business related. The funny thing is I never questioned it, just followed his leading. Apart from home economics, I loved my business classes as well. Today, I'm truly thankful because those very skills afforded me the livelihood to support my family as well as a gateway to my computer career and entrepreneurship.

Although we were having the time of our lives and life was good, our household wasn't a joyful or happy one when my dad was around. We lived in a beautiful two-story, four-bedroom, two-bathroom, split-level home, with a one-car garage, a nice backyard equipped with a large patio for entertaining, and child's playroom full of every toy imaginable, a child's paradise. But, as soon as we heard the garage door go up or the humming sound of my father's gold-with-the-black-top 1970 Sedan de Ville Cadillac entering the garage, my siblings and I would dash to our bedrooms and close the door for fear of what might happen.

My father was a stern, firm, crazy disciplinarian. He would come in the house yelling about whatever had happened, what was going to happen, or what was happening in his day. When he arrived in the house, you could hear a pin drop. Our house was always immaculately clean, hardwood floors buffed and shining. Everything was always in its place. You could smell the aroma of dinner throughout the house; my mother made sure of that. If I was out with my mother shopping or running an errand, when three o'clock struck, my mom was on the next bus home to prepare the family meal. There were times I found it quite annoying that we had to shorten our visit, shopping spree, or beach trip to run home to prepare dinner for my dad.

When my dad came home from work, if anything wasn't up to his par (which would change from one day to the next), he became furious, kicked butt, and asked questions two days later. I remember him being upset because I didn't empty the wastebaskets after school. He would use a fan belt off the car to whip me into shape. I would go to school the next day and my classmates would ask, "What are those black marks on your leg?" Looking down at my legs, I hadn't even noticed they were there. I would quickly swipe my tongue with my finger to use the saliva in an attempt to rub it off, but the grease marks from the fan belt didn't come off easily. I was so embarrassed and I didn't even realize what the grease marks were until I became an adult and reflected.

I could share many tragic experiences from between the ages of eight and fifteen for the trivial things I'd done or hadn't done. Like: forgetting to throw out the trash; for responding, "I don't know"; or for someone—whom I had no idea of their identity—who was calling the house and hanging up. I've been thrown down the stairs, kicked in the face, a glass ashtray thrown at me, and punched like a boxing opponent. I have migraine headaches to this day because of it and a few external scars.

In the midst of this emotional storm, my dad had the big idea to move down south. It was a culture shock and depressing at the same time. During that time, I felt so alone in all of this. I remember as a teenager feeling suicidal and scared, and I didn't know how to get out of that situation. Thank God I didn't know the first thing about hurting myself or where to go to research it. All I did was profusely cry out for hours in prayer to God to help me out of this circumstance. God made me strong, resilient, and forgiving. I was fifteen when He blessed me with an easygoing, jovial boyfriend who attended my church. During the latter part of my teenage years, God answered my prayers and gave me the relief I needed from the physical abuse.

I left my parents' home at the age of twenty, despite my parents saying otherwise. I couldn't take the yelling and living in fear any longer. My body was responding with a nagging stomach pain. I would leave home before my dad woke up and come home after I thought he had gone to bed to avoid the drama. I also severed my relationship with my high school boyfriend as well.

It was an experience living out on my own. I was lonely at first and remedied it with hanging out at the clubs. I met many people from all lifestyles. It was truly an awakening to see how other people lived, reacted, and coped with their personal situations. It was the first time I realized and appreciated the values my parents had instilled in me.

My six months of self-discovery halted. I met someone who became significant in my life. I had my first child at twenty-five and we were married when I was twenty-eight. Unfortunately, I was widowed after only thirteen days of being married. It was heart-wrenching to lose the love of my life in a car accident. I was mad at God for a while; I didn't understand why this had happened to me. Eventually, I learned to trust God's divine will for my life. After all, I had a son who was depending on me.

A year later, my friends kept advising me to go out and meet people. They saw I had become depressed. I took their advice and attended church, networking events, and social gatherings. One evening, I met a gentlemen who was dressed in a suit, very sophisticated in manner, and was extremely charismatic. Our conversation was quite jovial and intriguing. He took pride in telling me his father was a world-renowned entertainer. I really didn't believe him at the time. We exchanged telephone numbers.

A week went by and he called me, to my surprise. Our conversation lasted for about an hour. We talked about our families and backgrounds. He told me he loved me.

I said, "But you don't know me well enough to feel this way. How can that be?"

He proceeded to invite me out to an event. I met him there, and to my surprise, I met his world-renowned father along with other members of his family. It was a wonderful evening even though he didn't spend a lot of time with me due to him being a social butterfly. I spent most of the evening talking to his world-renowned father. We spent a lot of time together and our love grew for one another. A year later, I gave birth to my second child. It was a difficult pregnancy, and we began to have problems as a couple. Unfortunately, our relationship was severed.

Now, I was a single mother with two children, trying to work, pay daycare, instill values in my children, and deal with life's problems along the way. Only to God can I give the glory. I was reading a lot about being healthy. I changed my diet to vegetarian. I picked up the Bible and started reading it intensely. I became involved in a Bible-believing church and had my children in the children's ministries there. My youngest son's family was a godsend because they helped co-parent my children in their younger years. God, church, family, and career were our saving grace.

It was a family member who introduced me to a career opportunity in IT on a government contract that provided the stability we needed for our family for the last two decades. I thank God for the opportunity. Now, I have the means to pursue my entrepreneurial endeavors and God-given vision and mission to help women live their dreams out loud as they focus on improving their wellness, wisdom, and wealth. This is a Kingdom-building movement, Woman of Dominion, which God has given me.

What really ushered in this new movement I created was caring for my elderly parents. I earned my badge of honor of evolving into a woman of dominion while caring for them. Everything they'd instilled in me growing up about life contributed to caring for them. The coping skills I'd learn during the most tragic moments of my life gave me the endurance and commitment to be their advocate and to be compassionate. Here I was, caring for my mom in her final ten months of discovering she had cancer. It took an emotional and physical toll on me. The sleepless nights, battling with hospice care, and her husband's at-ti-tude were extremely stressful. I was also in a lot of physical pain that I totally ignored while lifting her and my father due to them not being able to do for themselves.

I was still scared of my father even in his feeble state, but I learned to overcome my fear by taking up for myself when he thought I wasn't meeting his expectations. I was never disrespectful or yelled at him, but demonstrated to him how I wanted to be treated. He eventually learned to be patient, especially after my mother's passing. He realized he only had his children to rely on.

My health was failing rapidly; I could no longer ignore the pain. I went to and fro looking for topical remedies for the joint and back pain. I changed my diet to a plant-based, no-sugar diet, detoxed every morning, and even went to a chiropractor. I was happy when I lost seventeen pounds in three weeks. It helped for a short while, but I made the mistake of skipping appointments due to work and travel. The pain grew worse and I couldn't walk as swiftly as before. I also noticed, if someone bumped into me, I would stumble. It would take thirty minutes to prepare a simple breakfast. I never told my dad how sick I was. He had already lost his sight, and I didn't want him worrying about my health on top of all the insecurities he was dealing with.

By now, my mother had passed. Although I was caring for my dad daily, I would carve out some time to decompress. This time, I scheduled a birthday girls' trip with my friends. During our annual trip, one of my dear friends asked if she could initiate a doctor's consultation after watching me suffer to do the basics of eating, dressing, and walking. I followed up after the initial consultation. After the visit, the doctor called me that afternoon. He said I had an advanced aggressive stage of rheumatoid arthritis. He also said, if I hadn't come to him when I did, I would have been in a wheelchair within two months. He prescribed medication and a referral to a rheumatologist.

It has been a year, and I have a praise report to share: I am doing ninety-five percent better than I was the day I walked in the doctor's office. I maintain a plant-based and sugar-free diet. I've also reduced my stress by walking out in nature and getting plenty of rest. Thank God for the most-beautiful friends. The lessons about self-care and being in the right community of people I've learned are to be treasured.

It's been six months since my dad passed and two-and-a-half years since my mother passed. I think about them every single day. I honored them until death, and I am thankful I was able to fulfil the hardest assignment God has given me on this earth. Now is my time to influence the world's wellness, wisdom, and wealth through the movement, Woman of Dominion. I've become a Certified Christian Financial Coach. My debut conference is this fall. Each quarter, I have planned an event. I am ready and excited to serve! Learn more at womanofdominion.com

Meet the Author

Martha Dodd has evolved into a woman of dominion. She arrived at this when she was speaking at her father's funeral. She felt she'd achieved an esteemed badge of honor because she'd honored her parents in their last five-to-seven years before transitioning. Everything her parents taught her as she grew up, along with the lessons and triumphs she achieved throughout her life, prepared her to take care of them during the most-vulnerable period of their lives.

This experience moved her into writing about her evolution and creating a movement for career women of faith. The movement educates, edifies, and empowers women in the areas of their wellness, wisdom, and wealth, hence, manifesting their dreams and living their lives out loud. People seem to find it hard to believe she is the mother of two and grandmother of three. She enjoys listening to God, learning about different cultures, cooking, sewing, entertaining friends, exotic travels, public speaking, and coaching.

To contact Martha Dodd:

Email: marthacdodd@gmail.com

Facebook: https://www.facebook.com/Woman-of-Dominion-1120530911403120/

Instagram: https://www.instagram.com/martha_dodd/

FROM VICTIM TO VICTORIOUS

by Kimbré Evans

Some people describe their childhood as fun and exciting. They share with you great stories of family vacations and awesome birthdays with sweet, loving, and joyous memories. Mine? Mine weren't so joyful. When I hear friends share some of their childhood memories, my heart drops.

My juvenile years were full of fear and pain. I gasp at the thoughts of the memories I carried in my heart for so many years. I walked around numb, yet bitter. Those memories made me hateful. I resented the people who had watched me be in pain and had done nothing. Most of all, I begrudged the ones who were happy because I didn't know how that felt.

It all began when my mother decided to marry a man who was in the church, portraying himself as a Christian. It seemed like the right thing to do, I guess. She was a single mother, and back then, that wasn't the most popular thing to be. I was a year old when my life took a drastic turn. Their marriage affected me in so many ways that it altered my life forever. At the age of two or three, he began molesting me. His obsession with me grew more and more each day. There were days he would molest me two or three times a day. At the age of five, he and another man decided to have me together. I remember crying as two grown men found pleasure in me as my cries were muted in their ears.

Soon he became a pastor and had his own church. For some reason, I thought this would change things, but they only got worse. He started making me go into his office before he preached; then he would call me a whore and a Jezebel during his message. The thrill of others taking advantage of me overwhelmed him. By the time I was nine years old, I had been sexually assaulted by four different people.

I was in so much pain. Physically, my body was numb, but emotionally, the pain was unbearable—so unbearable that I tried to commit suicide. That seemed to be the only way out of that dark place. The darkness was taking over my life. My mind could only hear what he said about me and remember everything he did to me. I hated him. I hated him so much that I called him Hitler.

When I turned twelve years old, I began to physically fight him off. He no longer had control of my body! I fought him with my hands and with my words. Eventually, he stopped trying to be sexually active with me. However, verbal abuse and beatings were his revenge. His words were like daggers in my heart:

"You ain't nothing but a hoe."

"No man's gon want you unless you sleep with them."

"You ugly and dumb."

"Ain't nobody ever gon love you."

These are the words he would throw at me all the time. He would wake me up in the middle of the night, beating me with a long leather belt with metal protruding from it, because the dishes weren't as clean as he liked. I was counting down to the day I could get away from him.

At church, he pretended to be saved and anointed, but at home he was hell. Bitterness and pain had taken full control of my life. I didn't see life as a gift. For me, it was nothing but a curse. I had learned to put on my mask and pretend that everything was wonderful, while my heart and soul were dying. I called it my church face.

Because I grew up in church, I knew all the church lingo. I knew when to wave my hands and when to shout Amen. Being privy to how the church operated, from the usher board to the pulpit, was easy for me. We went to church so much, it was our second home. Every day there was something at church we had to attend. This made me even more hostile. The hatred I embodied spilled over into all of my relationships. I couldn't have friends or close family because I not only lived in bitterness, I was also fearful.

I was so afraid of anyone new coming into my life that I kept them at arms' length because I didn't want to be hurt again. "My heart can't take any more pain" was something I repeatedly told myself. Anything that reminded me of the abuse would make me retreat emotionally, so I always felt alone—mostly because I put myself in a place to be alone.

For years I wore an emotional sign on my back that said, "Victim". It attracted pain and despair, so throughout my life that's how people treated me. I had children, marriages, and jobs, all while I operated in the church, feeling broken and in pain. I acted out the full role of a victim. It was toxic and happy people didn't want to be around me. I was contagious! My bitterness rubbed off on people and it wasn't good at all.

Looking in the mirror, I hated what I saw. Pain had taken over my body and formed in my face, and that was all I saw. But, as normal, my mask would go on my face and I would go about my day pretending everything was okay. I was far from being okay. I was dying inside and it was making me physically ill.

Suppressing the memories of what had made me so angry was part of my problem. Looking back on it, I now realize I suppressed them because whenever I told someone what my stepdad was doing to me, they would tell me to be quiet. I recall a preacher telling me, "Don't say that any more. He is a man of God, and no one will believe you anyway." I also remember the day during a testimony service at church that I stood up to testify. I yelled out that he was molesting me. Before I could finish, the evangelists and other ministers in the church had wrapped me up in a sheet, thrown me on the altar, and proceeded to try to "cast the demon" out of me. I was confused and crushed. After telling so many people and no action being taken, I suppressed the memory.

After so many years of feeling broken and pretending to be whole, one day I got tired. I was tired of hurting and being alone. I was experiencing nightmares, and so that I would not relive the trauma, I did everything in my power to keep from sleeping. My heart was extremely tired of hurting people who just simply wanted to love me. They say hurt people, hurt people. I know this to be so true. Finally, I wanted something different. Something other than being a victim.

I went to church one Sunday morning and couldn't function as I normally did. To some degree, there was something different about me, but I wasn't quite sure what it was yet. There was a restlessness in my soul. I was so dissatisfied with my life and I didn't know how to fix it. I sat in church that Sunday and cried. Not the normal victim tears. These tears were from a place I didn't recognize. The desperation of this cry was full of sincerity. All I knew was I needed help. I wanted to cry out to God, but I was so angry with Him. For years, I'd blamed Him for allowing so much pain to take place in my life. In my eyes, He didn't love me because He hadn't protected me. Nevertheless, I couldn't stop the tears.

No one bothered me the whole church service. They watched me cry, but I'm sure they didn't know how to console me. Afterward, I went home and lay across my bed. Still crying, I said, "God, if You love me, please take this pain from me." Then there were more tears. That night, I cried myself to sleep. This sleep was different. I didn't have a nightmare, I didn't wake up fearful of my stepdad being there, and I didn't need medication to put me to sleep. I had finally experienced a restful night.

The next day, when I woke up, I felt new. As I looked in the mirror, everything I saw that was unappealing to me, I asked God to let me see me through His eyes. I realized that morning how much I really hated myself. And, for the first time, I was able to pray wholeheartedly. No blaming anyone else. This wasn't about my stepdad or anyone else who had hurt me. This was about me. The focus had to be about my healing, and no one and nothing else. I needed help!

There were plenty of rough days. Some days I didn't want to get out of bed. Many days, I cried myself to sleep. I was similar to a drug addict. I was going through withdrawals because my heart and body had gotten comfortable being in pain. Comfort cannot coexist with healing and growth. God had to dig all those suppressed memories, the bitterness, and the hatred out of me. I had to relive it to overcome it. The very thing I had run from, God had me to face. I had to become emotionally naked.

The days of telling God I was angry with Him were plentiful. So many times I didn't have words, just tears. Each day He sent someone to show me He loved me. Strangers in the grocery store would embrace me, people at restaurants would pay for my food without me knowing who they were, and each time I would feel His love for me. The more I felt love, the less angry I felt about Him. After I acknowledged I was hurting and angry, I had to start on my road to forgiveness. Because I blamed me, I had to forgive me. I began to do something I call "Mirror Moments". I look in the mirror and tell myself the deep and sometimes painful things I need to hear. This time I said, "I forgive me! Kimbré, you are not what they did to you, and it was not your fault you were their target." After saying this over and over, I finally began to believe what I was saying.

I had to counteract what my stepdad had said to me. Even after so many years, his words still taunted me. I never had been in a position to receive love because I'd accepted the lies he'd told me. So I denounced every word he'd said and spoke the opposite. I am beautiful, lovable, intelligent, and worthy. Every day I'd say this to make my heart accept it.

Eventually, I began to look in the mirror and see a new Kimbré. Other people began to notice the change. Soon, I started gaining friends and people gravitated around me. I no longer possessed that hateful, mean attitude. Love and kindness began to take over my character. After thirty-eight years of living in fear, trauma, and bitterness, freedom was finally on my horizon.

On the road to forgiveness, I had to find room in my heart to forgive the people who'd hurt me. The hardest one to forgive was my stepdad. I prayed hard to forgive him. My thoughts concerning him were beginning to change, and once again, God had me to face it to see how far I had come. At a funeral, walking around to view the body, who did I come face-to-face with? Hitler (my stepdad) was right in my face. I took a deep breath, smiled, and kept walking. After years of not wanting to see him and hating him, I faced him with peace. I had never been so proud of me. It seemed like a small victory to some, but it was major to me. I was able to face the man who had hurt me and scarred my life. I went home and prayed for him. My prayer was that God would heal him. See, he had to be broken and in pain to do that to a child. Honestly, I can say I forgive him.

The road to forgiveness was long, but my next street toward healing was trust. I had to be able to trust God and others with my heart. I could not allow fear to control me any longer. Fear is not part of God's plan for our lives. I was afraid of everything. I had fear of commitment, fear of failure, fear of abandonment, and most of all, fear of rejection. It was paralyzing. I didn't apply for jobs I wanted, wouldn't sing or speak publicly, and didn't speak my thoughts because I was paralyzed with fear.

Since I had been so hurt at church, I stopped going for a while. During this process of healing, I felt the need to go back. It was difficult at first because I feared a pastor hurting me again. But I went. I started off going periodically, and the more I went, the more peace I felt. I found myself excited to go to church when I had dreaded going for so many years.

This journey was even tougher than the forgiveness. I had to face fear head on. I used Scriptures from the Bible. "Fear not" appears three hundred and sixty-five times in the Bible. Every day I would go for something and quote, "Fear not!" Day by day, it got easier. I had begun to conquer what I'd run away from. Because fear is a stalker, I still find the need to pull up a Scripture and remind myself. My life is no longer portraying that of a victim. I am now victorious!

Someone asked me, "How did you make it out?" My reply was, "I worshiped God the whole time." Worship is my sanity! Whenever I feel down, I worship God. I take my feelings off the throne and put them on the cross. I put God back on the throne where He belongs in my life. He doesn't deserve to be crucified again.

Whatever is holding you captive, you have the power to overcome it. Pain is not the end of your story. You are not what they did to you! You are not what they said about you! You deserve love and peace. He created you on purpose, for purpose, with purpose. Your dreams will not die! You are victorious! The next time you look in the mirror, I pray you will see yourself through the eyes of God.

God loves you and so do I!

Meet the Author

Kimbré Evans is the consummate example of a fighter. Overcoming obstacles others would have succumbed to, she has exhibited strength, courage, humility, and servitude that marvel even the wisest of men. She is a lifelong resident of Jackson, Mississippi, and the mother of three amazing children as she pursues her BBA at Strayer University. Her work ethic has made her a sought-after professional as she works as a recruiting specialist with one of the largest RPO's.

The daughter of a pastor, Kimbré learned that prayer will aid in her emancipation from pain and produces strength. She speaks loudly and displays her vehement passion for abused women and healing their inner scars through spiritual words of comfort. The fourth chapter of Ecclesiastes sums up her ministry: "Again I saw all the oppression that was done under the sun. And behold, the tears of the oppressed, and they had no one to comfort them!" (KJV)

To contact Kimbré Evans:
Email: kimelainespeaks@gmail.com
Facebook: Kimbre' Elaine

THE OTHER SIDE OF FEAR – UNWAVERING FAITH

by Staci A. Jackson Smith

From an earth-shaking diagnosis
that my body was attacking itself
to getting the gift of life from a "Perfect Stranger"

My name is Staci Smith. I'm a sixth through twelfth grade art school principal and middle school transition coach. I want to share my story with you about how I went from the shock and devastation of a heartbreaking diagnosis that my body was failing to getting the gift of life. The journey I went through not only provided me lifesaving medical treatment, it led me to face my deepest pains and fears of childhood, and to seek my life's purpose through the most unexpected circumstances. You never know what you can get from a stranger. I encourage you to hold on to these words: When you least expect it, the things that seem like they will crush you can build you up so you can help others for generations to come.

As a new mother, I looked into the eyes of my beautiful two-month-old son and was filled with a love I had never imagined was possible. Even in my joy, my life was about to change in a direction I could not have ever envisioned: the dreadful diagnosis that my body was attacking my kidneys from the inside out, as if they were foreign organisms! This news was terrifying on so many levels. Was I going to be able to take care of my new baby? What if my kidneys failed? Who would take care of him if I died? My son had a father and grandparents and aunts and uncles, but the thought that my child might not get to grow up with me, his mommy, was devastating! I reached out to all my praying friends in my time of crisis. My search connected me with one of my nurses who shared kidney issues.

In my state of fear, confusion, and panic, I completely forgot about my high school years when doctors had first looked at my kidneys as less than perfect. When I was seventeen years old, I had high blood pressure. It was my senior year and my family had moved because my dad got a job at a big corporation's headquarters office. I had just been elected as senior class president, and I had no desire to move anywhere, let alone from California to Connecticut! In spite of my attempts to figure out an alternative to moving, my parents and sister and I packed up our lives and made the trek across country. My parents took me to Yale University Hospital for a thorough exam of my kidneys. The iodine put in my veins to look at my kidneys made me feel like I was going to die! The test was not able to detect any problems with my kidneys at that time, so I forgot all about it until I got pregnant with my son.

I had a "high-risk pregnancy" because years of high blood pressure, in an otherwise healthy young woman, had caused my kidney function to deteriorate, but it only showed up in lab tests. Life was normal and I felt healthy. Because I could do everything I wanted in life and I looked well, I never allowed myself to "feel the pain" of my kidney disease journey. I didn't realize how serious it really was, so when it got worse, I honestly didn't grasp the seriousness of what was happening.

As soon as I got my diagnosis, I received a prayer that opened my ears to hear the voice of God. I could hear the words as if someone was speaking to me that I was going to be healed! I believed it wholeheartedly and went forward as if there was no other option!

No one would understand, but in my excitement, I told everyone who was praying for me to stop! You should have seen the reactions I got! God-fearing people were completely baffled and speechless, like the notion of me being healed of kidney disease was incomprehensible. Very few people could believe God had actually spoken to me, let alone was going to heal me! The looks of pity from those who thought I was delusional or completely nuts were combined with pleas to do something! One of those closest to me was angry and frustrated with me for stopping the process to get on the waiting list for a transplant! I'm sure he felt like I was accepting a death sentence! These were not the reactions I expected to my glorious pronouncement that God had personally told me, "The healing is done. It might not look like it right away, but the healing is done."

My family and friends were afraid for my life. I totally got it. Even though my daily activities seemed to be unhindered by the diagnosis, the pain and fear they felt were always present in their eyes. Without seeking the input of others, I began to turn every stone I could find in search of healing. One such stone was a naturopath, where I began a ninety-day herbal detox which was designed to cleanse the body of cancer patients down to the cellular level. Other stones included an internal medicine doctor who practiced traditional Western and several Eastern medicine regimens. My hope that each would be "the thing" to get my kidneys working fully again never waned. I even got "fired" by my nephrologist at Stanford Hospital because I didn't want to get a transplant when I first got diagnosed. I thought that was really funny. He was so frustrated with me.

After going through a series of non-traditional methodologies and having repeated life-threatening potassium levels which adversely affected my heart rate, my new nephrologist insisted I go on dialysis. My internal medicine doctor gently encouraged me to consider dialysis as a "detox for my blood". I reluctantly went into surgery to insert a tube into my heart so I could begin emergency dialysis. This wasn't at all what I had in mind, but I couldn't risk losing my life, not like this.

After "managing" my deteriorating kidney function for eight years, I became a dialysis patient. There are several types of dialysis, and at this point, I was on the most extreme type, where my blood was sucked out my body through the tube that was inserted near my heart, run through a machine to clean the toxins out of it, then pushed back in during a three-to-four-hour time span.

This was a huge blow to the picture I was holding in my mind and heart about my miracle, but I was left with no choice. As awful as that may sound, because I did not have the typical health issues of people on dialysis, like diabetes, I sat in my chair eating lunch, listening to music, or watching TV. I was even able to drive myself home! Most patients have to go home and get in bed after this process. This gave me a bit of hope!

After a month, I was able to switch to another type of dialysis I could do at home. I had to have another surgery to repair a hernia in my abdomen and insert a tube in a nearby area so I could deliver a sugar-water solution into my belly. Although this method required manually attaching a set of bags to drain and fill my peritoneal cavity six times every twenty-four hours, it was much better than going to a depressing dialysis clinic where people were so sick and suffering so badly. Friends helped me clear out space in my house to store the boxes of supplies. I got trained to do the process safely and correctly. My best Christmas gift that year was having the tube removed from chest! The three-or-four Lidocaine shots used to numb me didn't fully work, but I was determined not to have that tube dangling from my collar bone another day!

I became very efficient at doing my dialysis treatments while living my life. At night, I was able to use a machine that automatically drained and filled my abdomen while I slept. During the day, I could do my treatment while driving to pick my son up from school. I even got creative and figured out how to do a treatment at church during Praise Dance practice in the evening. My life, in some ways, revolved around doing the dialysis, but overall, I felt good. I still believed my miracle was coming and I never even considered going on a transplant list.

The hardest part of being on peritoneal dialysis was dietary restrictions. I couldn't eat cheese or ice cream, and got conflicting instructions on how much protein I should eat. I found out the hard way I was a food addict because I got very down when I couldn't eat what I wanted. My overall health was good for about four-and-a-half years; then I started feeling sick and very tired from the toxins building up in my system even with my dialysis treatments. I stopped urinating and having a period for about a year-and-a-half. It was becoming increasingly undeniable that my kidney function, or lack thereof, was starting to take its toll on my body and my life. I clearly remember praying and saying, "I think it's time for me to get a kidney transplant." Then I got very specific. "I think the person should be white, so I have less of a chance of getting the same disease and diagnosis. And I would like the person to be a Christian because they say you pick up traits from the person." I went on with my life and didn't give it a second thought.

On Thanksgiving morning 2007, at eight a.m., my phone rang. I sleepily answered, wondering who was calling so early. I heard the voice of a woman saying, I didn't know her, but she wanted to donate one of her kidneys to me. Suddenly, I remembered the words of my prayer about a transplant. Immediately, I knew it was the answer to my prayer as she shared it was also the answer to hers. She told me she wanted to donate a kidney to a single mom after seeing her fiancé, now husband, donate a kidney to his father when she was a single mom. We talked and I said I couldn't have surgery until the summer because I was a teacher.

It turned out this "stranger" and I were connected in multiple ways. Her best friend knew my sister, so they'd shared stories. My now "kidney sister" lived ten minutes away from my sister and they went to the same church. Her daughter and I share the same birthday. We later found out, while meeting at the hospital where her husband had donated his kidney, that we have similar personalities, church ministries, and taste in food when we ordered the same lunch several times as we did lab work. We got along great and our blood mixed perfectly! We were approved for the transplant!

Now that I had a living donor, I had to stay healthy until the summer when our surgeries were going to be scheduled. During the months leading up to the surgery, I had a friend whose husband died while on dialysis. It was a chilling reminder of how tenuous my condition really was. It was scary to think I had a condition that could end my life suddenly and silently. After all the years of treatments and lab work to monitor the levels of chemical buildup in my bloodstream that could cause my heart to stop or my bones to become brittle and the levels of fluid buildup that could drown me if my lungs filled with liquid if I took in more than I could drain out, I couldn't believe my miracle was happening!

Life was so precious to me over the thirteen years from hearing, "the healing is done", to being the recipient of a kidney from an unsolicited donor after never having been on a transplant list. I was ecstatic! My new kidney started working right away! I was able to go back to work four weeks after the surgery. The only pain medication I took was one Vicodin and it didn't even work. I was blessed to have no complications, and only felt better and better as time went on.

Looking back over this journey, I can say I was able to keep standing and keep going because I believed with every fiber of my being that God would do what He said He would do. It didn't matter what the doctors or anyone else said, or even how I felt. I didn't wonder, "Why me?", because I began to understand and believe I was chosen to walk through this experience as one who was given the gift of faith. I got to see how my faith increased the faith of people around me. My son, even though he was in elementary and middle school while all this was going on, wasn't afraid because he saw my faith and trusted his mom was going to be all right. My friends, family, and even strangers reacted differently when I told them my story and they saw me living out the faith I talked about with confidence; it was more than just words. I am forever changed through this experience.

If you are facing a challenge in your life of any kind, and have prayed and gotten an answer you heard like I did or read in the Bible—such as, "This sickness will not end in death. No, it is for God's glory so that God's Son may be glorified through it" John 11:4 NIV—or someone passed it on to you, believe it for your very life! Don't let your diagnosis define you. Utilize the "mind over matter principle" in which your body will follow your thoughts.

Be encouraged. Stay strong and positive. Have the faith to believe in your miracle. You never know what you can get from a stranger.

I learned that I not only experienced the miracle of the gift of a kidney, I experienced "healings" in relationships and other areas of my life for which I am eternally grateful and I honestly do not believe would have happened if my kidneys had been healed instantaneously. I learned to trust what I could not see and hold on to a belief that was not shared by all. It made me strong and fearless of the unknown.

Meet the author

Staci A. Smith is currently principal of Oakland School for the Arts. Ms. Smith entered the teaching field after fifteen years in corporate banking. As a second career, she provided over fifteen years of service to students as a middle school educator, math department chair, middle school assistant principal, and middle school principal.

Her combined experiences in the workforce and in her life-changing health challenges have led her to engage in coaching. She shares her insights and training as a middle school transition expert. Staci helps middle school teachers develop collaborative partnerships with parents, balance the demands of high-stakes testing, and support students beyond the classroom.

Staci is a published author, VIP member of the National Association of Professional Women and the National Association of Alumnae of Spelman College, where she earned a Bachelor of Science in Mathematics.

Her life statement is, "This too shall pass. Faith over fear."

To contact Staci Jackson Smith:
Email: MSTransitionXpert@gmail.com
Website: www.middleschooltransitionexpert.org

FROM RAGING STORM TO PEACEFUL WATERS

by Whitney Johnson

My journey from internal chaos to internal peace. I've always wanted a lifestyle of peace, a lifestyle devoid of chaos, internal toxicity, emotional overload, and self-doubt. I wanted to be able to walk into a room and be confident in my ability to let my light shine in a room where equal, if not more-impressive, talents and gifts were flourishing. I've always wanted to be vulnerable and strong at the same time. I've had this desire burning within me to shed the weight of other people's expectations, and to go forth and be who I am authentically. I've always wanted to know how to balance my goals with my relationships, my desires, and my dreams.

I struggled with wanting to become this woman for a long time, not realizing this woman was somewhere deep inside me. For a long time, I was this go-getter, overzealously chasing after my goals and dreams, so much so that my goals and dreams became my primary focus. Now don't get me wrong, I am still goal-oriented, but the difference is my focus has changed; my goals are no longer my priority. Making goals my priority caused my health to fail, it caused internal chaos, and it caused a lack of peace. I realize now that making my goals my priority was where I went wrong. Somewhere along the lines of making my goals my priority, I lost my inner peace. I lost the ability to self-regulate. My anxiety increased and so did my stress level. I got to a point in my life where I realized something had to change.

Then one day I discovered the beauty of making myself the priority. It was crazy. The day I started making myself the priority, my entire life changed internally. I know that by society's standards people judge you by what you have going for you on the outside, but neglect the fact that you may be internally in chaos. However, I've come to know that being okay internally always trumps external appearances. Since the day I started to make myself the priority, I have been able to walk in peace and confidence without caring about the opinions of others. I wasn't always at this place. Let me take you back to a time when my life shifted. I didn't know what was happening to me then, but hindsight is twenty/twenty. I can see how this exact moment turned me into the extremely goal-driven individual I was.

On September 13, 1999, at approximately five a.m., my little sister came running into my room. "Whitney, Whitney, get up!" She nudged me to wake up. I asked her, "What's wrong?" and she said, "Momma fell on the floor and she isn't waking up!" I rolled out of bed to go see what she was talking about. I got to my mother's room and saw her lying on the floor, not moving. I called her to wake up. "Momma, get up." She didn't move. I nudged her and still she didn't move. I started to panic. My eleven-year-old senses were telling me something wasn't right. I hesitantly hit my mother with a little force and she didn't move at all.

I knew I should probably call 9-1-1, but I was scared. I picked up the phone and called my uncle. I frantically recanted the situation to him. He told me to immediately hang up and dial 9-1-1. I called 9-1-1 and they asked me to check for my mother's pulse… There was no pulse. Not wanting to give up hope, the 9-1-1 operator coached me on how to perform CPR on my mother. I did the best I could before the ambulance and paramedics arrived. When the paramedics arrived, they escorted me and my sister out of the room. Sometime later, a family member came to tell me and my sister that my mother had passed away.

At that moment—I didn't realize it then—I began to suppress the nurturing side of me. My nurturer, feminine role model, best girlfriend had died. Most of my teenage years were filled with accomplishment, after accomplishment, after accomplishment. I was in more organizations and afterschool activities than I care to name. I realize now that is where I found my self-worth. I felt valuable when I accomplished things. I felt empty when I didn't. I carried this goal-chasing spirit into my college career and became a first-generation college graduate.

Now I'm not saying accomplishing goals is bad, that's not what I'm saying at all, but the spirit behind the way I was accomplishing my goals was bad. I didn't feel valued on my own. I realized I was desperately missing the nurturing feminine touch of a mother. While all of my friends were getting weekly calls from their mothers, I wasn't. While my father was in the picture and he did an awesome job as my father, he still wasn't my mother. There are certain nurturing capabilities only a mother can give. And vice versa, there are some things we need as women that only a father can give.

Sometimes, if we are missing either factor in our lives, it can cause us to become off-balance. For some people, they become too vulnerable, open, giving, because they are searching for something to fill that void. I was just the opposite. I became tough, closed off, and lacking empathy. My goal-focused life was devoid of vulnerability, divine femininity, and peace. I was going through life with force, not with flow. Everything I did was extremely task-oriented, and my relationships and health suffered drastically.

When I was in college, I became sick. I mean so sick I couldn't eat, and not only could I not eat, I could barely walk. Where it normally would take me five-to-seven minutes to get across campus to a class, it started to take me fifteen-to-twenty minutes. I was easily out of breath, and I was having crazy, consistent heartburn. Something was wrong! I went to the doctor's office on campus. The doctor ordered a colonoscopy. I was only twenty-two! What-the-heck did I need a colonoscopy for?

I called my dad. My dad gave me some encouraging words and he and my stepmother came down for my colonoscopy. Thankfully, the colonoscopy was clear. However, the doctor asked me an important question.

"Are there any traumatic experiences that have occurred in your life?"

I thought about it and said, "Yes."

He asked me about the experiences.

I said, "The death of my mother."

He said, " Hmmm… okay… All your colonoscopy results are clear and your bloodwork is good. Maybe this is a time in your life where you feel like you really need your mother."

Y'all, I completely dismissed that thought. I hadn't even been thinking about my mother. He then offered me some medication. I didn't take the medication, but I also didn't get the message. If there is one piece of advice, I could give you right now, it would be, slow down. Don't be so focused on your goals that you ignore the warning signs your body, friends, relatives, or even doctors may be giving you. If you aren't careful, your internal chaos will turn into external manifestations.

There were a few other times in my life where I was sick and my internal chaos manifested as chest pains, headaches, and weight gain. After two or three times of things happening that couldn't be explained by doctors, I began to do my own research. During my research, I found that stress, worry, anxiety, and fear can psychosomatically manifest itself in various ways. Anytime you have excessive stress, worry, anxiety, and fear, you have internal chaos.

If you have ever found yourself in a place where you know you are in internal chaos—maybe you are experiencing some anxiety, maybe you have some depression, maybe you are overeating and can't seem to stop, maybe you are so goal-driven that your relationships are suffering—I know the feeling. I know what it's like to be achieving things externally, but still feel like things aren't right internally. Because I know what it feels like, I don't want to leave you hanging. I want to give you three keys you can implement right now to help shift you from a place of internal chaos into a place of internal peace. These are the exact keys I used to obtain inner peace and confidence, and to radiate hope and love.

The first key I want to give you is: Detox

When I say detox, there are three areas I'm talking about specifically that I focus on and I tell my clients to focus on when detoxing. The first area is social media. Detox from social medial. Social media can put so many unexpected pressures on us that it's best to stay off for a while when you're trying to remove internal chaos. Social media is also a time-sucker. Oftentimes, people spend hours a day scrolling though social media when they could make better use of their time.

The second area is sugar. Detox from sugar. I don't care how you do it, just do it. I suggest starting with seven days. Take a seven-day break; then go back and do a twenty-one-day sugar detox. Sugar is an addictive substance and there are a lot of the foods we eat that contain sugar. Sugar and the foods we eat that contain sugar affect our mood. You will often find that detoxing from sugar will automatically help improve your mood, and it will cut out a lot of drinks and foods you buy that also contain added chemicals other than sugars that also affect your mood.

The third area is negativity. Detox from negativity. Negativity can be found in the shows you watch, in the people you hang around, in your work environment, and in your home environment. For some people, detoxing from negativity will be easier than others; nevertheless, it is still something that needs to occur. When you detox from negativity, you allow space in your mental capacity to be filled with things that actually bring you joy. When people come to you with negativity during your detox, keep the conversations short and sweet. You don't have to be rude, but you do have to change the subject or excuse yourself from the conversation.

The second key I want to give you is: Practice Acceptance

Accept whatever role you have to play in you not being happy. Your external goals don't mean a thing if you aren't satisfied on the inside. Sometimes, we try to avoid feelings and emotions, so we bury them under work, family, relationships, etc. When you practice acceptance, you no longer give yourself permission to stay in internal chaos. You thoroughly assess where you are and how you got to where you are. Then, you accept that it's okay not to have it all together. It's okay to not know your exact next move. It's okay to be human.

The third key I have for you is: Release Control

Inhale. Exhale. Let go. Oftentimes, we try to hold on to things that are causing us more harm and damage than they would if we were to let them go. This step has been the most beneficial step in my journey, and I find it is often the most beneficial step in my clients' lives. It will take some practice at first, but once you get used to letting things go, the easier it becomes. If you implement the keys, I have shared with you, you will be well on your way to living a peaceful, fulfilling life—a life devoid of chaos. Your internal raging waters will turn into peaceful, calm waves. If I can go from being internally chaotic to internally peaceful, then, my sister, you can too.

Meet the Author

Whitney Johnson is an author and licensed clinical social worker who was born and raised in Jacksonville, Florida. She attended the University of Central Florida, where she attained a bachelor's in Psychology and a master's in Social Work. She still lives in Jacksonville today, close to her family.

Despite enjoying her career as a mental health therapist, Whitney has decided to take her message of inspiration, motivation, and hope outside the office. She is a dynamic public speaker and success coach who teaches women how to overcome mental and emotional blocks to success.

When she has time to relax, Whitney enjoys live music, going to art festivals, game nights with friends, and keeping fit. She also loves to travel whenever she can, both within the United States and abroad.

To contact Whitney Johnson:
Facebook: www.facebook.com/wjohnsononline
Instagram: WhitneyJohnsonOnline

FROM CANCER TO COMEBACK: HOW MY FAITH MADE ME WHOLE!

by Lisa Yvette Jones

"...the chastisement of our peace was upon Him;
and with His stripes we are healed!
(Isa. 53:5b, KJV)

Wow! April of 2009. My life was going so amazingly well. I was happy. I was in this blissful state of basking in that peace that surpasses all understanding. I cannot explain it, but for some reason, I was floating on cloud nine. I was enjoying my life as a newly-divorced mother of one, our son Anthony, who was having the time of his life while completing his first year of high school as a boarding student at the prestigious Cranbrook Kingswood High School in Bloomfield Hills, Michigan. My career was advancing more than I had imagined. My mother, the now-late and great Queenie Victoria Thompson, was doing well after surviving a stroke in February of 2009, and I was enjoy being G-Ma to my goddaughter

Brandi's two little boys, my god-grandchildren, Chosen and Jordan. They are such handsome young men. They now have a new little brother Jeremiah and he is such a cutie.

As I was going about life and welcoming a new year of life, I had another reason to thank God for His unfailing love: my birthday, April 12th. Later that month and as another gift to me, I decided to have my yearly exam—you know, ladies, the one each of us looks forward to having—that yearly Papanicolaou (Pap) smear/exam. Yes, that one.

Somewhere between my birthday and Mother's Day, I began experiencing a tranquil, calm state of existence that was truly beyond anything I had ever imagined and I did not know why. In fact, I did not care to know why; all I knew was I never wanted that experience to end. It was so blissful! Everything was going well. Then I received a call from my primary care physician. She advised me to stop by her office because she had something she wanted to "share" with me.

During my visit, she advised me that the results of my yearly Pap smear/exam were abnormal, but it could mean anything and I should do anything but worry. She referred me to an obstetrician/ gynecologist, aka Ob/Gyn. For some reason, the news did not shake my core at all. I was still at peace. I believe I was beginning to find out so much more about how God prepares and protects His dearly-beloved children.

The Ob/Gyn and I met. She examined me, then she advised me that she believed it was best to refer me to a gynecological oncologist. I asked if she saw cancer. She said, "Only a biopsy and a pathological report can confirm such." She was quite professional and kind. I thanked her and her receptionist made the appointment for me. Whatever she told them was serious enough for them to see me the next day.

I next met with my oncologist. He was very kind and gentle. As he was examining me, he asked if I planned to have any more children. It was at that point I realized something more was going on, but I still refused to be shaken off my core. I refused to allow my faith in God and His promises to fail me. It was up to me to keep the faith and not doubt Him.

After the biopsy and other tests, I finally received another call while at work on May 19, 2009—"the call" from the oncology nurse that initially shocked my world! Without telling me the reason for her call, I was advised that my surgery was scheduled for the following Monday, May 25, 2009, at six a.m. I found the news quite perplexing because no one had spoken with me since the biopsy.

I inquired about the surgery and what it entailed. To the amazement of the nurse on the other end, she was not aware that I had not been informed of my diagnosis. Without inquiring if I was alone, at work, or able to speak about this health crisis, she informed me that I had been diagnosed with a very aggressive cancer of the cervix, Papillary Serous Carcinoma of the Cervix to be exact. She further informed me that I was already in Stage 3 with a high grade of this deadly disease, and that if I did not have the surgery as soon as possible, it would continue to spread.

Now, I have to admit, hearing that news for the first time in my tranquil world was a bit unnerving. In fact, a tear almost came to my eye, but I would not allow it. I then informed her that I needed to meet with the doctor before any surgery. She understood and apologized profusely. She scheduled the appointment with the oncologist, and he too apologized profusely. He then answered all my questions. But guess what? As tragic as the news of this deadly disease they claimed was growing rapidly inside me, I was still at peace. What?! Only God can give you the peace I was experiencing.

I requested a second and third opinions. The doctor understood, but advised that if I did not have the surgery soon, I would die. I looked the doctor in the eyes and said, "Doctor, I respect you as a doctor, but what I cannot have, is you speaking death over me. If we are to continue in this partnership, you will need to change your vocabulary to speak words of life over me; otherwise, I will find a doctor who will."

He said, "Very well, but I have been in this position for a very long time, and I have seen this type of cancer. It is quite aggressive and vicious. In fact, I have never seen anyone survive this cancer once it reaches their main organs."

I told the doctor he had never met me before and I come with a team (Father, Son, and Holy Spirit) that would make him a believer in miracles yet. I said to him, "With God, all things are possible!"

He said, "As you believe."

I knew it was time to fast and pray even the more fervently. I thought, 'What sense would it make to have come this far by faith, leaning on the Lord, but when I need Him the most, to begin doubting Him? No! I need God more than ever.' I called on a few prayer warriors I knew could get prayers through. I called on my now-late ex-husband Anthony, Mother Laura Heard, and Evangelist Tammy Young. I thought at least one family member should know what I was facing. The process of who to tell in my immediate family was much more arduous than I'd imagined!

I couldn't tell my mother this news about her daughter because she was still recovering from a stroke. I didn't want to take the chance of the news about me having a residual effect on her healing and recovery. I couldn't tell my son because he was studying for his finals and I didn't want anything to disrupt his studies or his full ride to Cranbrook. If I had thought I wasn't going to be around to see him graduate high school, I would have told him, but my faith already had me on the other side of that ugliness called cancer!

I couldn't tell my sister Tracie or my brothers Raymond, Bryan, Calvin, or Dwaine because they wouldn't have taken the news well at all. I needed someone who could be strong for me and who would keep my news confidential until I was ready to tell them. I called my brother Duane, pronounced (da-wan), aka Bawse, and shared the news with him. He was shocked, but I knew he wouldn't tell anyone, not even our dear mother. If you ever want your secret kept, tell my brother Duane.

The results were in from my second pathological report and they were the same. I needed surgery and quickly. The only request the second oncologist had was, "ASAP or else!" He further advised that I needed to choose either him or my other doctor because time was of the essence. He indicated, not only was my entire cervix covered with the cancer, they also saw spots on my ovaries and my uterus. It was their belief that the cancer was aggressively spreading.

I thanked the doctor and left. I knew it was time to shut everything and everyone out while I fasted, prayed, and shut in with God. I went on a three-day fast on nothing but water, prayer, praise, trust, faith, and the will to live and not die! The fight was on! But guess what? I was still at peace! It was so beyond my understanding that I knew God was in the midst of my battle.

Day 1: The peace of God was so powerful, I believe satan was pulling his horns out his head.

Day 2: I refused to give in to any doubt, fears, or the taunting of the enemy. I stayed before God and in my Word. The more I prayed, the more I praised, the more I read my healing scriptures, the stronger, more confident, and ready for the fight I became.

Day 3: My true purpose was revealed! Ah ha! This was what the enemy was after. He went through all that to distract me from what God was about to reveal to me. What a loser! While I lifted a praise to the Lord that woke up my entire neighborhood, the Lord revealed He had called, chosen, and was sending me into the ministry. He also revealed the diagnosis was not unto death, that I should live and not die, and that it would never return again! Hallelujah! Immediately, the fast was lifted!

I then called the original oncologist. He wanted me to have surgery as soon as possible. In fact, he scheduled it for June 1, 2009. I told him not so. My son wasn't due to take his finals until the following week. The surgery would have to wait until he completed his finals. In fact, I advised him that June 29th was a convenient date for me. Besides, my Chief Physician had already spoken my outcome, and He had already stopped the spreading of that deadliness inside me. I was living my outcome, not what I was going through!

My oncologist said, "If you do not have the surgery by June 1st, you could die!"

I stood up, looked the doctor in his eyes, and said, "I have already consulted the Chief Physician and He said, it is not unto death, the spreading has stopped, and it will never return again."

He asked if I had gone over his head to the chief doctor at the hospital. I replied, "No, but I went to the Chief Healer, Deliverer, Savior, and King—My God! Now, are you the doctor everyone claims you are? Are you the one folk in medical schools are reading about? Are you the claimed genius of this type of cancer? Well, if you are, then buckle up for the ride and handle my surgery, but if you believe you cannot, Doctor, tell me now so I can find a doctor who is up for the challenge!"

My doctor looked at me and said, "You are one stubborn patient!"

I replied, "No, Doctor, I am one steadfast patient! I will see you on the 29th of June."

He said, "Indeed you will."

June 29th came! It was time to remove the cancer. The physical surgery was successful because the supernatural surgery had already taken place! The cancer was and is forever canceled! Today, I am a living, breathing, walking, talking, blessed woman of God who lives in the peace of God that is beyond my understanding, and so can you!

Trust God today with your situation! He is waiting to give you peace in the midst of your storm. When you trust Him with everything you have, I promise, you will never be the same. You will bounce back after a setback and people will have a hard time understanding it because you will not look like what you have been through. Glory to God! The health challenge setback was only a setup for my greatest comeback!

Here are a few non-negotiable nuggets that helped me through then and they are keeping me today. From Cancer to Comeback, take these steps:

1. Pray! Begin your prayer with: (James 5:13)
    - Praising God Almighty!
    - Reflecting on all He has already done for you.
    - Adoring Him, His goodness, His Grace, and His Mercy.
    - Yielding fully to the presence and the power of communion with God.

2. Trust God and His Word! If you believe God is Who He says He is, then trust Him! (Proverbs 3:5-6)

3. Demand partnership/inclusion in your health care with your medical team!

4. Know your core circle, your community of support. Embrace them and allow them to embrace you through your challenge.

5. Listen to your body, i.e., your sudden cravings, your mood changes, etc.

I began to have an unquenchable desire for berries. My body went into attack mode against the cancer. According to the National Cancer Institute, antioxidants protect cells from damage caused by harmful molecules called free radicals. Antioxidants are known to slow the growth and prevent the further development of cancer (driscolls.com/retrieved 09/17/2018).

6. Know what keeps you grounded and centered. My

f.a.i.t.h. (Forsaking All, I Trust Him) made me whole! Which is why I had joy like a river and peace like a fountain.

7. Never take your health for granted. Schedule and keep all appointments. I had no symptoms!

8. Steal away for some serious alone-time to pray, meditate, journal, and quiet your thoughts so you can be fully attentive to you and to God.

9. Celebrate your comeback by having an attitude of gratitude! Talk about your victories, celebrate life, and walk in your purpose without asking permission, but by giving notice to the world that you are present and accounted for.

As for me, I am destined to finish the work God has assigned for me and so will you! I truly believe, if the unexpected diagnosis of Stage 3 High-Grade, Papillary Serous Carcinoma of the Cervix was going to keep me from my God-ordained destiny, God would never have allowed it to happen to me.

I am a woman of peace, gifted to Encourage, to Inspire, and to Empower! Dying an early death was non-negotiable; therefore, I shall live and not die!

Cancer was put on notice and canceled!

Meet the Author

Minister Lisa Yvette Jones was diagnosed with Stage 3 High-Grade Papillary Serous Carcinoma of the Cervix on May of 2009. She had no symptoms to warn her of this vicious attack! Surgery or die was what the medical community advised her. But God! This woman of faith would not hear death sentences pronounced over her life because she knew The Divine Healer of her body and the Anchor of her soul—Jesus! Hallelujah! Her F.A.I.T.H. (Forsaking All, I Trust Him) and the PEACE of GOD were her mantra.

Minister Lisa is employed as a public servant and has established Peace Beyond Understanding Ministries. She holds a bachelor's in Business Administration, a master's in Counseling, certification as a John C. Maxwell coach, teacher, trainer, and speaker, a Dale Carnegie-trained public speaker, a contributing writer for Prayer and Praise online magazine, and a community ambassador with the American Cancer Society, to name a few.

To contact Minister Lisa:

Email: peacebeyondunderstanding@outlook.com
Telephone: (248) 973-7684
Facebook: Lisa Yvette Jones
Twitter: @LisaYvetteJone1
Instagram: lisayvettejones2

MAMA SAID THERE WOULD BE DAYS LIKE THIS

by Lavonia Perryman

Growing up was filled with annual basketball events, school plays, dance classes, piano classes, and weekly trips to the library. One of my first books was Shakespeare for Kids. By the time I was fifteen, I had read all of Shakespeare's works. Both of my parents are avid readers too. And to think, Daddy only had an eighth-grade education! Mama graduated from college and taught for forty years. In fact, as a black family, neither my mother nor I was the first to obtain a college education. We have four generations of college graduates. It's been years since I graduated from college, however, I am now preparing to attend Harvard. In the meantime, I am doing what I love, hosting a weekly talk radio show in Detroit. Between shows, I manage my media relations and communications training company.

As I look back now, I was destined to be on radio and

TV. You see I was the first little black girl to dance on Detroit Channel 7's Auntie Dee's show. Keep in mind, I was only five or so. I didn't even know I was on TV; I was just doing what my mother told to me do. She would say, "Dance, Vonia, when the red light comes on." Was I good? Yes! I was also on the popular Detroit Saturday morning children's show Milky's Movie Party Show. I was one of the kids who helped the clown with his magic tricks. I had no clue what he was doing, but I was having fun. Again, I had no idea I was on TV.

I performed throughout the city, and my mother will tell you, at times, she had to come on stage to get me off the stage because I would continue to play the piano or dance even when the music had stopped. When I was around nine years old, I produced and starred in my first play, Betsy Ross and the American Flag. I wrote the play, identified the actors, and produced the play. I built a stage in the alley; that's right, in the alley. You see, Grandmamma Samantha lived downstairs and we lived upstairs, and our house was right next to an alley.

Like in many families, Christmas was the fun holiday, full of family, friends, food, and gifts. In my house, we also put a great deal of attention on the spiritual side. Again, I took stage—in the church. During one Christmas when I was a little girl, I was chosen to be the Virgin Mary in the Christmas play. Yes, I was first little black girl to play Mary in the predominantly-white school. This would only be the beginning of my firsts; for example, the first black woman to have an official girls' basketball camp in Michigan.

I had never attended public school and I so wanted to go to Cass Tech High School, where all the kids who were destined to rule the world attended. I wore a uniform to school every day, my shoes either loafers or black-and-whites, but I never felt out of place. I was okay with all of that, because at St. Cecilia's, I was considered to be one of the talented, creative, and intelligent students.

I was the oldest of five, two girls (myself and Linda Jean) and three boys (Alex Jr., Ronald, and Nehemiah); we all attended St. Cecilia's. My family wasn't well off, but Mama and Daddy worked long and very hard, sometimes two and three jobs, just to make sure their children had what we needed and sometimes what we wanted. I've been blessed to have both of my parents still in my life. Mama is ninety-two and Daddy is ninety-four. That's the best blessing a girl can have, next to her health and a loving mate.

Blessings have been many, but oh, along the way, some painful knockouts. It was on a Christmas morning almost forty years ago that my life took a deep dive into the canyon of pain, horror, misery, shock, sadness, and confusion. In that moment, I changed, which changed the way I looked at the world, people, and myself. Oh, I was hurting; my soul had been ripped into pieces. You see, I received a call Christmas morning 1979 that my sister had been killed by a drunk driver. I can't tell you what I heard. All I know is that my husband of five months, Dr. Johnnie Fairfax, said something. I don't remember the words, but I got the message: Your sister was hit and killed in Detroit. By this time, I was living in Washington, D.C., anchoring the evening drive news (a major spot for a journalist) on the Mutual Black Network.

Before that, I was in Detroit working at WCAR radio as a reporter and hosting a show on WTVS Channel 56,

Detroit Black Journal and Detroit Black News. I was having ball—dating and working a dream job. Here I was in Detroit, named the Michigan Media Woman of the Year. Dating talented young men who were either star athletes, awesome entertainers, promising elected officials, or upcoming lawyers. Here I was, working with some wonderful people and had a boss whose family had actually adopted me! Then I was spotted by the general manager of Mutual Black Network, which was a dream job in a major media market. I moved to Washington, D.C., thinking I might be there for a year or two. No, I was there for nearly thirty years. I was born and raised in Detroit, but D.C. is in my heart and I miss it.

The year was full of joy and pain, and I was enjoying every moment. Joy because I'd met the guy I was going to marry; pain because I just couldn't find the wedding dress I wanted and I was running out of time. Here I was, a little girl from the westside of Detroit, a little black Catholic girl who'd attended St. Leo's and St. Cecilia's. I seemed to fit D.C. and D.C. seemed to fit me. But while in D.C., what I thought would be a place of smooth sailing became a place where I learned the bumps in the road of life sometimes are hills and mountains. I am here to tell you, losing my sister was my mountain I didn't think I would be able to climb.

Here I'd lost my sister, buried my sister during the Christmas holiday, then was back to work in two weeks. People didn't know what to say, and guess what? Neither did I. So everybody just went back to the work-and-play routine, but I am here to tell you, I'd changed. I just didn't know how much. My actions dictated how people treated me. So, people tiptoed around me, made concessions. I don't believe I was always nice. Some swear up and down I was, but I do know, if I didn't get my way, I wouldn't talk to you for days—I mean, not one word. A sign of crazy, wouldn't you say?! I did this on numerous occasions.

I worked every day, even on Sundays. I also played hard—after work, I would party—but I found joy in working in the community and politics was my drug. All my life, I have been involved in media, politics, and entertainment, and I found a way to merge these three where they made sense to me, so I opened the Lavonia Perryman Media and Communications Training Center that is active today. I think my sister would proud of me. I still miss her every day. When I lost my sister, I did not hesitate to become the guardian of her two girls, Shawnda and Virginia, nor did my husband. I believe God has angels on earth and He assigns them to people like me—people who He knows will need support, love, and help in the time of crisis. Think about it: I meet a guy when I get to D.C., marry the guy in July, speak to my sister in September, when she says if anything happens to her take care of her girls, then I lose her in December.

I now know it was tough for him with three women who were in mourning and didn't know it. Lesson learned.

Time went on and I was knocked down again; my baby brother Nehemiah died. Then a few years later Ronald, another brother, died. Sadness took over, but I attempted to press on with my life. I often wondered how my parents lived through those tragedies.

Life is a journey with roads of joy, pain, mistakes, success, and love. Major personal work has gone into my healing from trauma, discovering my divine self-love, and self-determination. All of this finally led to celebrating family, friends, and me. We can all go from pain to power. Here are the lessons I have discovered about life, love, career, and family:

Lesson One: You must remember that one is able to stand strong in the face of danger. I learned that from Mother. My mother is the engine that powers my life.

Lesson Two: Do you and do what makes you happy, satisfied, and full. As Nike says, "Do it now." Don't wait until you're fifty. Live life with gusto now.

Lesson Three: Happiness doesn't come from being better or prettier or thinner or smarter. It comes from enjoying life in the moment.

Lesson Four: Don't be afraid to pursue your own style. Fashion is not frivolous. It is a form of self-expression. Sparkle and shine with style.

Lesson Five: Appreciate every age group; all have something to celebrate.

Lesson Six: Be charitable with time. Help the needy. Teach the young. Protect the innocent.

Lesson Seven: Seek joy.

Lesson Eight: Women should exercise their power more. Have the courage to buck the trends when your values are violated.

Lesson Nine: Don't be in fear of money. Money is not evil. Start early in building wealth. And, yes, save for a rainy day.

Lesson Ten: I learned from my father, do your best to hang in there when times get tough and trust in God. He's got your back.

Lesson Eleven: Malcolm X once said: "Education is the passport to the future, for tomorrow belongs to those who prepare for it today."

Lesson Twelve: Women of color are significantly underrepresented at all levels of government. We must show up and show out on the local, state, and national political levels.
Lesson Thirteen: The systems of oppression are active. We must stay "awake".

Lesson Fourteen: We must give voice not only in the church but in the streets. I don't think I ever saw Mother Teresa in the pulpit. I always saw her in the street with the people, taking some action to make someone's life better. That's the life I will continue to attempt to live. A life of planning, studying, and action. One that will take me from hidden pain to power.

Meet the Author

Lavonia Perryman has found success in front of the TV camera and behind as the president of Lavonia Perryman Communications, Media and Technology Training Institute. She trains local and national political candidates and celebrities on media relations. In addition, she has produced several award-winning TV programs, including Emmy-awarded America's Black Forum.

Presently, Lavonia is also the host of the 910AM radio program, The Lavonia Perryman Show.

In 2016, Lavonia served as the Women's Vote Political Director for Hillary Clinton. Prior to this, she served on President Barack Obama's Detroit Transition Team.

Lavonia's company's clients have included the Democratic National Conventions in the 1990's and a press secretary in President Clinton and Al Gore's Presidential Transition Office. She still manages media relations for Reverend Jesse Jackson at the Rainbow PUSH Coalition Michigan Office.

Lavonia is the recipient of several awards, one being Detroit's Women in Radio and Television, Media Woman of the Year.

To contact Lavonia Perryman:

Email:lavoniaperryman@gmail.com
Telephone: 313.404.0977
Website: www.910amsuperstation.com
Mail: Lavonia Perryman
Communications, Media and Technology Training Institute
415 Burns Drive, Suite S707, Detroit, Michigan 48214

INSECURITIES

by Brenda Puckett

Imaging growing up in a world where you could leave your doors open at night. It was a time when your neighbors cared about one another and looked out for each other. It was peaceful, with much love floating in the air. I want to give you a synopsis of the time and era of my beginnings, take you back to a place in my life many years ago to share with you my journey of how I overcame my insecurities from my childhood.

I grew up in a small town in the 60's where neighbors were like family. If you needed sugar, you would send your child next door for a cup of sugar. The cost of bread was twenty-two cents. A gallon of gas was thirty cents. A dozen eggs, fifty-seven cents. The movie theater was a quarter. Milk was delivered through the milk door on the side of the house. It was a time when kids could play outside all day long, until the street lights came on, giving them an indication it was time to go in the house.

I remember coming home to get in front of the television screen to watch my favorite shows in black and white. There were no computers and no cable. When the TV station went off-the-air for the night, you would hear a loud sound and the screen would go blank. It was a time when we were saddened by the death of President Kennedy and our Civil Rights Leader, Martin Luther King, Jr.

I grew up in a family of seven: mother, father, myself, and four sisters. My parents came to Detroit from Mississippi in an effort to search for employment opportunities. My mother was a Susie Homemaker, meaning her only job was to stay home and take care of her husband and children, of which I am the youngest.

I remember going to Mississippi to visit my grandparents on their farm every summer when the school year was completed. My father would take his three youngest daughters back to Mississippi on vacation every summer. One day, my grandmother decided to take me to town to shop. I saw a water fountain and went over to drink from it, not able to read the sign that said, white only. I was scolded so harshly, I cried profusely. I was very young and had no idea about segregation, but I learned quickly.

One day, while we were riding on the wagon, my papa said to my sister and me we could own the mules that were pulling us. I was so overjoyed, not knowing he was just saying it to make us smile, yet inspiring us to be entrepreneurs. We would often milk the cows and feed the pigs. I also had the experience of picking peanuts under the hot, heated sun.

Most of my young life was very happy. Even though I was considered the baby of the family, I really didn't get the attention that comes with it. Dad was at work during the day and Mom was always busy cooking, cleaning, and sewing. We looked forward to Sunday when the family would get dressed up in our very best clothes and head out for church. The best days were when we would go swimming at the school during the summer.

One day, while taking swim lessons, I was in the pool on the deep-water side and the teacher got an important call. She demanded we hang on to the edge of the pool until she returned. Well, I decided to disobey and let go to see if I could tread on my own. Needless to say, I got caught and had to go back to the shallow water. Because of being disobedient, I haven't learned how to tread water to this day.

I guess you are asking now, "When did your insecurities begin?"

They actually began when I was five and beginning my first year of school, when my mother was told by my teacher that I talked too much. That was the first time I had heard anyone say bad things about me. I really didn't think I talked a lot, but I was only five. That was the first of many years of feeling inadequate. I believe that was the beginning of my insecurities.

I can remember getting teased by some of my sisters. I was told one night, "Girl, you were so black when momma brought you home from the hospital, she had to take you straight to the tub to bleach you, then scrub the blackness off you." Needless to say, I really believed it. I would look at my skin after coming indoors from a hot summer day and say to myself, "I am so black."

I often admired girls I saw on television who were on stage dancing. I didn't look like them, so therefore, I considered myself unattractive. If that wasn't bad enough, one day, I was told, "You look like a monkey." I was truly flabbergasted after hearing that one. At night, I would cry myself to sleep, and when daybreak came, I would avoid looking in the mirror.

Understand this: Our family joked a lot and teased each other often, so, around the time I reached ten years of age, I considered myself to be very ugly. But it wasn't all bad because I remember going out in the backyard and smelling the rose bush, picking flowers, and pulling tomatoes off the vines of Momma's garden bush. I loved to play out there, sometimes along with my friends as we ate penny candy. I had a best friend who seemed to not care about how I looked or how much I talked. Denise and I remained friends until she passed at the age of thirty-two.

As I grew older, I kind of learned how to defend myself, but I still felt the hurt and pain of the earlier years.

Do you remember when I said I was told I talked too much when I began school? I guess it quieted me down, because when I started my career, I was told I didn't articulate my words. The problem with this is, if a person is fed negativity all their life, sooner or later the seed that has been planted will produce deep roots. For many years, I thought I couldn't articulate my words, I was ugly, and my skin color was too dark.

Even though my parents took me to church from birth, it wasn't until I turned twelve that I accepted God in my life, but because I was young, I began to stray away from being active when I became an adult. One morning, I woke up and realized there had to be more to life than what I was seeing. I went to church and heard that God loves me, and I am beautiful and wonderfully made. I found out I was more than a conqueror and I could do all things through Christ who strengthens me. I began to start believing in myself.

One day, while gazing out the window at the business where I worked, I realized I was created for a reason and there was a divine calling on my life. I knew there was purpose in me, and I had not tapped into the many gifts and talents. As I looked over my life, I discovered that if I continued to look back, I wouldn't look forward to see all of the potential lying dormant inside me. I realized if I wanted change, it had to start with me. I found out, as a man thinks, so is he, so I changed the way I was thinking. Once I did that, my life started taking a turn.

It's amazing how, if we change the way we think, we change the course of our future. I began to realize I had allowed what people said about me to affect my mind and my thinking. Once this happens, your course in life is predicated on what others say about you and not what God says. I was an introvert in character probably because of magnified words that were meant to destroy me.

I began to believe in myself and have positive persuasion through positive thinking, I was determined to change the course of direction in my life. I came to find out, when you believe in yourself, others will believe in you. However, you don't need anyone to validate you. I had to realize there were gifts and talents in me. There are gifts and talents in us all. I believe we are here to help others discover what's inside them as well, and if we lose the battle of confidence, the battle of insecurities will be won.

We have to know who we are as well as to Whom we belong. The Creator of the universe has taken the time to uniquely create us. We have to believe in ourselves. We have to believe He didn't make any mistakes. We can't believe what others say about us. We have to believe what God says about us.

As the years went by, I developed a concern for those who are less-privileged and who are poverty-stricken. Doors began to open as I walked into the calling on my life. I noticed that others are also suffering with all kinds of insecurities. It could be financial, marital, mental, or emotional. When I thought about it, I realized we all need encouragement at some time in our life.

I began to reach out and touch the lives of men, women, and children of all ages and all walks of life. What they all had in common was the need for pure and unconditional love. We all need love in our lives, but we need to love ourselves before we can love someone else. We were created out of love; therefore, it is essential that we walk, talk, and pass love to others. I believe behind trouble youths lies a lack of love they either don't feel or don't know how to receive.

The gateway to becoming an overcomer is recognizing there is a problem and allowing yourself to totally heal through the process of loving yourself as well as loving others. It is essential we recognize our worth and validity, and that we do not succumb to the negative forces that want to steal our joy. We must know we can be free from any insecurities through the power of the mind. We have to have a renewed mind and renewed strength. We have to let go of all negative influences and hold on to positive people. If we spend too much time with the naysayers, eventually, it will take hold and we will become what we associate with.

There are many gifts and talents in us that have not

been discovered. Our knowledge and experiences in life can take us to heights that can change our environment and even change our world. We should not be afraid to step out into a position of authority according to the level and degree of our faith. We are as high as our faith can take us. If we can believe the impossible, then nothing is impossible, and we can prosper in every area of our life. We don't have to fear or worry about being all we can be. Have you ever heard the sky is the limit? Well, if we transform our minds into thinking and believing in ourselves, there is absolutely nothing we can't accomplish.

I was a little girl who was so intimidated and had little faith in myself. Now, I am the CEO of a nonprofit organization that has served thousands. I believe in myself through God who has made me in His image and likeness. It is certainly a beautiful thing to walk in your calling and to fulfill the purpose God has intended for you.

There is a time for everything, and it is time for us to get up and step out in faith and be all we can be. Again, we are created out of love, and if we are created out of love, shouldn't we exemplify love? There is much work for us to do.

Again, you are wonderfully and beautifully made. Don't allow anyone to make you feel uncomfortable in your own skin. You are beautiful! Never forget it.

Meet the Author

Brenda Puckett is a Christian speaker and the CEO and Founder of Vessels of Charity Outreach Ministries, Inc. Her ministry is headquartered near the Detroit suburb of Southfield, Michigan.
Brenda was born in Detroit, Michigan. She and her husband have four adult children. Currently, she is a chaplain for the Detroit Police Department and has a passion for serving her community. She retired from an electric company after thirty-two years, with outstanding awards for service, and began working with The Word Network.
Brenda's dream is to change one life at a time by motivating individuals to fulfill their purpose and mission in life.

To contact Brenda Puckett:
Mail: PO Box 2027, Southfield, MI 48037
Email:vesselsofcharity@gmail.com

NEVER GIVE UP STARTING OVER WHEN YOU ARE OVER FIFTY

by Shurvone Wright

When you've given your life to a career for thirty-one years, you just never think you're going to do anything different, but when you're faced with a decision that could change your life forever and the lives of those you love, it's a very scary place to be in. It's a place where you have to decide to stay stuck or take the leap of faith and jump into the unknown.

However, I have learned when you are faced with a decision that can change the course of your life, you find a strength and courage you never knew existed. I've always had an inner strength and knowing that I would be something greater in my later years; I just did not know exactly what that would be.

In my transition and starting over in a new profession, I have learned I can do all things through Christ Who gives me strength, I have learned how to trust that small voice in my head and heart that guides me daily. I have learned that I am more courageous than I thought possible and more outspoken, which has given me a newfound strength. I have learned that turning inward, getting quiet when faced with a hard decision, has so much power. These newfound skills and knowledge has helped me start again after fifty. I am a woman who loves to help and motivate others. I believe I was placed on this planet to inspire others to grow and change.

I was born and raised in the San Francisco Bay Area. Life was not always easy for me. I was faced with many challenges as a young lady, seeing things and experiencing things that changed my life. I was a very shy and insecure young woman, but again, always a deep knowing there was more for me to do. I just did not know what. When I was twenty-one years old—another life defining age—I was faced with a decision to live or die. I was doing things and living a life that would have led to my demise if I hadn't gotten out of that fast lifestyle I was living. I remember lying in bed, depressed and filled with the unknown, and as clear as day, I heard a voice say, "You are going to die if you don't stop now." That day was the day that changed my life forever and began the journey of my nursing career of thirty-one years, and where I am today.

When my nursing career started at twenty-one years old, I just knew I would practice as a nurse until I retired. I quickly learned how much I loved caring for, helping, and educating people on their care, working in the nursing profession gave me many opportunities to do what

I loved. I worked in the hospital, clinics, home-care settings, drug and alcohol rehab, finally landing in the office setting where I loved to work as nurse behind the scene, reviewing and authorizing services for patients. I really thought I would retire from that job. It was comfortable. I had amazing co-workers I called friends and life was good. I was getting a great paycheck. It was at this job that God started to prepare me for where I am today and the confidence-building journey.

During a worksite counseling session I requested to help me get over being scared to speak up in meetings and to be bold enough to stand my grounds in a professional manner, the counselor asked me how I thought others saw me. I rattled off all these amazing, positive things, which she wrote on a whiteboard. Then she asked, how did I see myself, and to my surprise, the list was very different. She then said, "You need to learn how to be 'Confident Without Regret'." In that moment, my life changed. The light bulb came on, my life flashed before me, and I became very emotional because it was like I finally had permission to own who I was and not be afraid of others' opinions. It was okay to love myself right where I was and along the way to where I was going. That day was the day my movement was born. I knew God was going to do something with it; I just did not know what.

So I returned to my desk and quickly wrote "Confidence Without Regret" down and decided I was going to trademark the name, which I did. It took a year, but I did it. When God gives you something, don't sit on it; move and He will guide you every step of the way.

Shortly after that experience, the homey type of environment of the workplace started to feel very corporate and a less-desirable work environment. Then layoffs happened and I decided I wasn't going to wait around for them to lay me off. I was going to start looking for a new job. So, I found a new job and things started off well, and I thought, *'Okay, I can do this.'* Then things changed when I got a new boss. My work environment became very toxic, to the point my doctor put me on medical leave.

Once that happened, I knew I was at a crossroads again in my life where I needed to make a very difficult decision. When I am faced with a very challenging decision in my life, I have learned to pray, listen, and wait on God. *What do you have in place when you are faced with difficult decisions? Do you get scared? Do you freeze up and not do anything? Do you just wait and hope all things are going to work out?*

So during my prayer time as I was sitting at home, I remember thinking, *'Lord, what am I going to do? I cannot go back to that toxic workplace.'* Again in the moments I needed clarity, I heard in my spirit, "call John a financial professional" I could not believe what I was feeling. I had never talked to him about that career and he'd never approached me in the three years we'd worked together in the community with the Chamber of Commerce. I was shocked but I listened because I know such a drastic change from nursing to being an insurance agent could not have come from own thoughts; plus, I was fifty-two years old and I would be starting a new career. I would be starting in something I knew nothing about. I also knew I could never give up on myself and my ambition.

So I called him and set up an appointment, which turned into three appointments with me and two with my husband to make sure I was doing the right thing.

After beginning the process of onboarding and studying for my licensing exam, I realized how much I loved what I was learning about the insurance industry and how I could use this information to help people. Then it dawned on me I was helping people treat their financial situations instead of their health situations; so, again, I was still helping and educating others. *When you are in the midst of making a big change, look for how it fits in the core of why God placed you here and that will certainly help you decide if you are going down the right path.*

I finished all the required onboarding and I was ready to schedule and take the exam to become a licensed life insurance agent. I started to get nervous and make excuses in my head. "I can't do this." "I am going to fail the test." "I am not a good test taker." So, needless to say, I canceled my exam the day before, crying to the person who'd helped with the onboarding process

Have you talked yourself out of something new and exciting? Have you gotten so scared of change you decided to not change and to stay comfortable?

That is what I almost did—stay comfortable and miserable in a job I had come to hate. However, the counsel I received was to just step back, believe in myself and go for it, and to not give up, because if I did, I would never know the outcome and never know what I could have accomplished. I rescheduled my exam and passed on the first try. I was so happy and excited to know God had confirmed what I was supposed to do, even with the little fear that had set in. I knew I had made the right decision.

Once I started this journey and I started going to meetings, a little fear set in and I remember telling myself, "Never give up!" and, "Turn off the fear in your head!"

I was so intimidated by the entire process that I decided I had to do better, be better, perform better in all areas. I didn't know how I was going to do that, but I just knew I had to. I knew I had to develop a stance to Never Give Up !

It wasn't easy. It was a daily process of conquering my fears. I learned how to meditate on a daily basis, in the morning and at night. I had to pray and work at remembering all the things I am grateful for. I decided to not let fear control me and that this new career had to work; there was no other option for me.

When you take that stance in your life, you start to see issue as opportunities to grow. You see more options and ideas to make things work. I also decided that, whenever faced with bad days, I would never give up on anything! I would pray and meditate and believe that things would be better, and they did get better. You have to develop a belief in yourself that's stronger than your fears. You have to decide, no matter what, you are going to make it, and watch what happens. Surround yourself with positive people, and people who will encourage you and guide you.

In my first year as an agent, I achieved a certain sales goals and was invited to attend an annual meeting honoring professionals who achieved this goal. I also earned multiple awards my first year.

I monitor my feelings and make a conscious effort to switch off the nerves, intimidation, and feelings of being overwhelmed. It's an ongoing process, and I have worked hard to become the woman I am now.

You too have to work hard at never giving up, going after your dreams, and always knowing you have something to offer the world.

In light of all I have gone through in the last year and a half, I started a closed Facebook group called Women's Empowerment Ministry Confidence Without Regret with over three hundred forty women, I had my first Women's Conference in 2017, with over eighty-plus women in attendance, all wearing the T-shirt I'd designed for them that said "Confidence Without Regret" This group helps to encourage women to live their best life and to be encouraged to love themselves along the way.

This last year has taught me to believe in myself and dream big, and to always remember I am capable of accomplishing anything I set out to do. I have learned how to control how long I allow any given situation to affect me, and how to move on and conquer my fears whenever they try to rear their heads. I have learned that starting over at fifty-two has been challenging but so very rewarding. I feel like nothing is impossible. So many amazing things have happened and more is to come.

My business is thriving. I am now an author. I am traveling. I was featured in a company publication directed towards women due to my production and networking skills. I will soon travel to another one of their offices to train other agents. All because I decided to not let my fears hold me back and fly above the storm.

Are you facing a big decision in your life? What fears do you have to overcome to move forward with that decision?

I would encourage you to first slow down long enough to think about what you really want!

- Don't be afraid to dream big! God would not give

you big dreams and not give you the skills and resources to accomplish them.
- Make a vision board and add your goals with dates to the board. It's okay to update the board keep your goals updated.
- Find what works for you to get through your day when faced with challenges, such as prayer, meditation, or other tools and resources.
- Decide that it's okay to start over at fifty if that's what you decide to do, and learn what it takes to believe you can achieve anything.
- Make a plan, get into a routine, and stick to it.
- Be Persistent, Consistent, and Never Give Up!
- Be your own best cheerleader!
- Surround yourself with like-minded people and get a mentor.

I wouldn't ask my readers to do anything I haven't done and/or I am continuing to do. I can ask you and encourage you to do these things because they have all proven to work for me. However, you have to find what works for you and make it apart of your life.

I hope you were able to at least take one thing away that can change your life and the way you look at taking a leap of faith on your dreams when you are over fifty.

I want you to walk away knowing you can re-invent your life. You can start a second profession when you are over fifty and be successful.

I also want you all to realize that many people have a second career in their lifetime, so don't be ashamed or hesitant to go after your second profession. There's nothing wrong with wanting to explore other options after you turn fifty. Just make sure you have a support system in place, whatever that looks like for you.

Blessings and encouragement from me to you as you explore what's out there in this amazing world. Never, never give up!

Happy Exploring,
Love to you all,
Shurvone Wright

Meet the Author

Shurvone Wright, an entrepreneur, owns a small business financial practice specializing in helping business owners. Using insurance as a foundational component, she also helps client families prepare for the future by protecting and preserving what is important to them. Her efforts and business acumen have earned recognition with several awards all in one year.

A previous thirty-year healthcare career in nursing provided her an avenue to launch a lifelong commitment of helping others.

She started a private Facebook women's support group called "Confidence Without Regret" that helps women build confidence and courage on their journey through life.

Married for twenty-five years to Roger Wright, they have four daughters and three grandchildren. Shurvone Wright and her family reside in Brentwood, California.

Shurvone Wright
Contact Information for Speaking Engagements
Phone: 510-435-3649
ConfidenceWithoutRegret@gmail.com
Facebook: Confidence Without Regret

Made in the USA
Middletown, DE
14 August 2019